Benefits and Earnings Losses for Permanently Disabled Workers in California

Trends Through the Great Recession and Effects of Recent Reforms

Michael Dworsky, Seth A. Seabury, Frank W. Neuhauser, Ujwal Kharel, Roald Euller

For more information on this publication, visit www.rand.org/t/RR1299

Library of Congress Cataloging-in-Publication Data

Names: Dworsky, Michael, author.
Title: Benefits and earnings losses for permanently disabled workers in California :
  trends through the great recession and effects of recent reforms / Michael Dworsky,
  Seth A. Seabury, Frank W. Neuhauser, Ujwal Kharel, Roald Euller.
Description: Santa Monica, CA : RAND, 2016. | Includes bibliographicalreferences.
Identifiers: LCCN 2016038605 | ISBN 9780833096319 (pbk. : alk. paper)
Subjects: LCSH: Workers' compensation--California. | Workers'
  compensation--Law and legislation--California. | Disability insurance
  claimants--California. | Employers' liability--California.
Classification: LCC HD7103.65.U62 C238 2016 | DDC 368.4/1--dc23
LC record available at https://lccn.loc.gov/2016038605

Preface

California adopted sweeping reforms to its workers' compensation system in 2012 under Senate Bill (S.B.) 863. Motivated in part by concerns about whether wage replacement benefits for injured workers receiving permanent partial disability (PPD) benefits were sufficiently generous, the reforms included several changes intended to improve the adequacy of PPD benefits. S.B. 863 also required the California Commission on Health and Safety and Workers' Compensation (CHSWC) to conduct a study "to compare average loss of earnings for employees who sustained work-related injuries with permanent disability ratings under the schedule."

This study, which was sponsored by CHSWC in order to meet the statutory requirement, is intended to describe trends in the economic consequences of permanently disabling injuries in the period (2005–2012) between implementation of the last major reform legislation to affect California's workers' compensation system and the enactment of S.B. 863. Because this period spanned the Great Recession of 2008–2009, we analyze in detail the negative impact of this economic downturn on outcomes for injured workers. We then measure trends in disability ratings and benefits over this time period and predict the likely influence of S.B. 863 on the adequacy and equity of PPD benefits.

The intended audience includes policymakers in the California legislature as well as the broader community of stakeholders who are directly involved with or affected by the California workers' compensation system, particularly workers and employers. Many of the issues raised here, in particular our analysis of the influence of the business cycle on outcomes for disabled workers and the adequacy of benefits, may be of interest to policymakers involved with workers' compensation in jurisdictions beyond California.

A draft version of this report was posted online for public comment from March to April, 2016. As of October 6, 2016, the resulting comments can be accessed at http://www.dir.ca.gov/chswc/Reports/2016/Wage_Loss_Public_Comments.pdf

RAND Institute for Civil Justice

The RAND Institute for Civil Justice (ICJ) is dedicated to improving the civil justice system by supplying policymakers and the public with rigorous and nonpartisan research. Its studies identify trends in litigation and inform policy choices about liability, compensation, regulation, risk management, and insurance. The institute builds on a long tradition of RAND Corporation research characterized by an interdisciplinary, empirical approach to public policy issues and rigorous standards of quality, objectivity, and independence.

ICJ research is supported by pooled grants from a range of sources, including corporations, trade and professional associations, individuals, government agencies, and private foundations. All its reports are subject to peer review and disseminated widely to policymakers, practitioners in law and business, other researchers, and the public.

ICJ is part of RAND Justice Policy within RAND Justice, Infrastructure, and Environment, a division of the RAND Corporation dedicated to improving policy- and decisionmaking in a wide range of policy domains, including civil and criminal justice, infrastructure protection and homeland security, transportation and energy policy, and environmental and natural resource policy.

Questions or comments about this report should be sent to the project leader, Michael Dworsky, an associate economist at RAND (mdworsky@rand.org). For more information about the RAND Institute for Civil Justice, see www.rand.org/icj or contact the director at icjdirector@rand.org.

Contents

Figures

Tables

Summary

Introduction

In 2013, California began implementing major reforms to the state workers' compensation system that were enacted in 2012 as part of Senate Bill (S.B.) 863. One of the key goals of S.B. 863 was to increase the generosity of permanent partial disability (PPD) benefits awarded to permanently disabled workers. The increase in benefits was motivated by a widespread perception that benefits were too low to provide adequate compensation for the earnings losses experienced by permanently disabled workers. To monitor the success of S.B. 863 in accomplishing the goal of improving benefit adequacy, the California Commission on Health and Safety and Workers' Compensation (CHSWC) contracted with the RAND Corporation to assess recent trends in earnings loss and PPD benefits and how injury compensation will be affected by S.B. 863. The purpose of this report is to present those findings.

The benefit increases enacted under S.B. 863 may be viewed in part as a policy response to reductions in impairment ratings and benefits that followed implementation of a major reform package enacted in 2004 as S.B. 899. This bill contained several provisions that effectively reduced the generosity of benefits. A previous RAND study estimated that, in the two years following the enactment of these provisions, average indemnity benefits for permanently disabled workers fell by roughly one-third compared to the average that had prevailed before S.B. 899 was implemented (Seabury et al., 2011). As a result, the *replacement rate* of lost income—the fraction of lost earnings replaced by indemnity benefits—fell by roughly one-fourth.

S.B. 863 used several distinct policy levers to increase benefits. First, S.B. 863 raised both the minimum and the maximum weekly wage to be used in calculating PPD benefits for the first time since 2006. Because most workers had earnings above the weekly maximum wage, the 26-percent increase in the weekly maximum wage, implemented in two steps between 2012 and 2014, was anticipated to have a particularly large effect on benefits. Second, S.B. 863 eliminated what was known as the *future earnings capacity* (FEC) adjustment, a factor that was used to adjust the disability ratings for certain types of injuries. Elimination of the FEC was accomplished by setting the FEC for all injuries to the maximum value allowed under S.B. 899, yielding higher ratings for all impairments that previously had an FEC factor below the maximum.[1] Third, the reform created a new benefit called the *return to work* benefit to be funded at $120 million per year. This program offers supplemental payments to injured workers whose permanent disability benefits are considered disproportionately low in comparison to their earnings loss.

---

[1] The bill also prohibited compensation based on certain controversial types of secondary (or *add-on*) impairments (e.g., sexual dysfunction or sleep disorder), though, if anything, these changes reduce benefits for affected workers.

All of these changes would clearly increase benefits, but the size of the reforms' effects on benefits might vary substantially according to an injured worker's circumstances. For example, the increase in the maximum wage might lead to a 26-percent increase in benefits for a worker with wages above the new maximum while having no effect on benefits for a worker with wages just below the old maximum. Increases in ratings and benefits brought about by the elimination of the FEC would vary widely across different types of injuries. The return to work fund, meanwhile, was explicitly designed to target workers with the most severe earnings losses. Because these provisions had the potential to affect different groups very differently and had the potential to interact in complex ways, the ultimate influence of S.B. 863 on the generosity and fairness of benefits is impossible to predict without detailed analysis.

This report follows past RAND work and examines the changes to workers' compensation policy in the context of empirical estimates of the lost earnings experienced by permanently disabled workers. Estimating earnings losses is the only way to judge how the S.B. 863 benefit increases compare to earnings losses for the average permanently disabled worker. Careful measurement of earnings losses for permanently disabled workers is particularly important for assessment of California's recent PPD reforms because the period following enactment of S.B. 899 and leading up to passage of S.B. 863 spanned the Great Recession of 2008–2009, the most severe economic downturn in the United States since the Great Depression. In order to understand the baseline levels of earnings losses and benefit adequacy against which to evaluate S.B. 863, it is necessary to examine whether the recession and recovery have led to differentially poor labor market outcomes for disabled workers.

Research Objectives of This Report

This report provides policymakers and stakeholders with evidence about the extent to which the benefit increases enacted under S.B. 863 have improved compensation for permanently disabling workplace injuries. This information is needed to assess whether PPD benefits compensate workers at an adequate level and whether benefits are delivered in an equitable fashion across different types of workers and injuries. To provide this evidence, we pursued the following research objectives.

To measure the replacement of lost income, we estimated the earnings losses and statutory benefits for permanently disabled workers in California who were injured during the eight years (2005 through 2012) leading up to implementation of S.B. 863. We estimated the average earnings lost due to permanently disabling injuries that occurred over this period, spanning the end of the housing boom and the Great Recession of 2008–2009. In particular, we examined in detail the impact that these economic events had on earnings losses of permanently disabled workers. We also measured trends in impairment ratings and statutory benefits in order to evaluate, for the first time, the adequacy of PPD benefits at the time that S.B. 863 was enacted.

While we provide evidence on how these reforms have affected disability ratings and statutory benefits for the earliest groups of workers to receive disability evaluations under S.B. 863, it remains too early to observe the long-term consequences of injuries occurring after the implementation of S.B. 863. We therefore evaluate the effectiveness of the reforms to PPD benefits enacted under S.B. 863 by estimating how these reforms *would have* changed the adequacy of benefits for workers injured over the period leading up to the law's enactment. Finally, because S.B. 863 changed benefits in part by modifying the disability rating system, we also evaluate the effect of these changes on the equity, or fairness, of PPD benefits.

Summary of Key Findings and Implications

The remainder of this summary and the full report document our findings in detail. Here we offer a brief summary that outlines the key findings and their policy implications.

- Permanently disabled workers injured after the beginning of the Great Recession experienced much more severe earnings losses than workers injured before, suggesting that the economic downturn disproportionately affected injured workers relative to uninjured workers.
- For the average worker who was injured between 2005 and 2012, the benefit increases enacted under S.B. 863 would have significantly increased replacement rates of lost income compared to what they were under S.B. 899. Specifically, we estimated that the portion of after-tax earnings losses replaced by benefits would have risen by 21.4 percentage points, from 58.8 percent to 80.2 percent.
- While S.B. 863 will lead to higher benefits, much of this benefit increase is offset by the increases in earnings losses that followed the Great Recession.
- Both changes in ratings and increases in the maximum weekly wage led to substantial increases in benefit adequacy, while the return to work benefit had a more modest effect, on average. However, the return to work benefit had the largest effect on wage replacement rates for the lowest-wage workers. Since the other provisions of S.B. 863 led to larger benefit increases for middle-income and high-income workers, the return to work benefit has an important role to play in preserving the progressivity of PPD benefits.

These findings have several important implications for California policymakers. We found that earnings losses for permanently disabled workers are highly sensitive to the business cycle, reinforcing the need to understand the context of economic conditions when assessing benefit adequacy. We also found that the Great Recession had a disproportionately negative impact on permanently disabled workers, with relatively little recovery by 2013. Careful monitoring is needed to assess the generosity of S.B. 863 as economic conditions change. Also, more should be done to develop effective strategies and policies for tying benefits to measures of economic conditions such as return to work, to help ensure that the adequacy of benefits does not rise or fall dramatically when underlying economic conditions change.

We also found that the return to work benefit serves a policy objective that is not advanced by the other S.B. 863 reforms by making PPD benefit compensation more progressive. Even though it has a modest effect on overall wage replacement rates, the fact that the benefit was targeted to the lowest-earning and most at-risk workers—those who do not return to work after an injury—led to an overall increase in the progressivity of benefits. However, more needs to be done to monitor the take-up and use of the benefits and to ensure that the return to work benefit continues to support the most at-risk workers.

Finally, our analysis suggested that the changes to benefits brought about by S.B. 863 had little effect on the overall equity of disability benefits across different types of injuries. While it is reassuring that eliminating the FEC did not make benefit delivery substantially less equitable across types of injuries, we found that the FEC itself was not a very effective tool for making benefits more equitable: inequities in ratings and benefits between workers with different types of injuries were widespread in the period before S.B. 863, even though the FEC was designed to eliminate such inequities. Our analysis suggests that these inequities will continue under S.B. 863. More work should be done to address these inequities using empirical data on systematic differences in earnings losses across different workers.

Measuring Earnings Losses for Permanently Disabled Workers

The policy questions posed in this report center on earnings and employment losses, impairment ratings, and benefits among permanently disabled workers. We measure these outcomes by analyzing administrative data from several state agencies using the matching methodology developed for numerous prior RAND studies for CHSWC, including Peterson et al. (1998); Reville, Boden, et al. (2001); Reville and Schoeni (2001); Reville, Schoeni, and Martin (2002); Reville, Seabury, et al. (2005); and Seabury et al. (2011).

The earnings loss caused by a permanently disabling workplace injury can be defined as the reduction in a worker's earnings relative to what that worker would have earned if the injury had not occurred. An injured worker's actual earnings history can be observed directly using administrative data on earnings. The challenge to estimating earnings losses comes from estimating what a worker would have earned in the absence of an injury. Workers may experience changes in earnings for a variety of reasons unrelated to injury, including wage growth or promotion, job changes, retirement, or unemployment. Simply comparing an injured worker's earnings before and after an injury would ignore these other factors and attribute all changes to the injury. Accurately estimating the earnings loss caused by an injury requires estimating the so-called *potential earnings*, the hypothetical earnings that injured workers would have received absent the injury. We follow past RAND studies and estimate potential earnings by matching injured workers to uninjured "control" workers who worked at the same firm and had very similar earnings prior to the injury. The earnings of these control workers in the time period following the injury serve as a natural estimate for the potential earnings of their closely matched injured workers.

Our data in this study are similar to the data used in past studies (e.g., Peterson et al., 1998; Reville, Seabury, et al., 2005). Workers' compensation claims data are linked to earnings data for claimants based on their Social Security number, and this information is combined with earnings data to identify the control group. We use data on workers' compensation claimants from two sources: the Workers' Compensation Information System (WCIS) and the California Disability Evaluation Unit (DEU).

The WCIS, which was developed and is managed by the Department of Industrial Relations (DIR), collects information at the individual claim level from claims administrators reporting to the DIR. These data represent an important source of information for analyzing and evaluating the California workers' compensation system that is likely to be representative of paid claims for the private sector. The DEU is a unit within the Division of Workers' Compensation that takes information from medical reports and uses it to produce a disability rating, a number from 0 to 100 indicating the severity of disability that, in turn, is used to determine PPD benefits. The DEU ratings include precise data on all elements of the rating, and we use this detailed information to simulate S.B. 863 ratings and benefits for those injured under S.B. 899.

Conclusions

We found that the benefit increases brought about by S.B. 863 have done much to restore compensation for permanent partial disabilities in California to levels not seen since before the 2004 reforms. Replacement rates under the new statutory rules under S.B. 863 should rise significantly, even in the face of a relatively sluggish economy in which the earnings of disabled workers continue to lag behind their pre-recession levels. We also found that the return to work benefit did little to influence overall benefit adequacy, but it is expected to target benefits toward the most at-risk, low-wage workers, increasing the progressivity of PPD compensation. Nevertheless, several issues remain that require ongoing monitoring of return to work and earnings losses, and some systemic inequities remain in the system that should be addressed in future studies and reform efforts.

Acknowledgments

We are grateful to the California Commission on Health and Safety and Workers' Compensation for funding this research. We also wish to thank Eduardo Enz, who served as the executive officer of CHSWC during the course of the project, and Irina Nemirovsky, Research Program Specialist at the Department of Industrial Relations, for their support. We thank the individual commissioners for providing us with feedback, and the many staff members at CHSWC who provided us with input. Christine Baker, director of the DIR, was a valuable source of input throughout the project, as was Amy Coombe in the DIR Director's Office. Thanks are also owed to the many stakeholders (including employers, labor, insurers, attorneys, and others) who shared their input and knowledge about the functioning of the workers' compensation system with the authors. The empirical analyses at the core of this report would not have been possible without the cooperation and generous input of many CHSWC and DIR staff members. Liza Dizon worked assiduously to extract our analytic data from the WCIS and transfer it securely to RAND, and Cheryl Swope and Debra Lofing of the Employment Development Department were always responsive and helpful in helping us extract wage data from EDD. Glenn Shor and John Gordon patiently addressed many questions about the details of the WCIS. Kathy Patterson and Barry Knight provided critical insights into the use and interpretation data from the Disability Evaluation Unit. A number of other DIR and CHSWC staff also shared their expertise with us throughout the project, and we wish to thank all of them. Alex Swedlow and David Powell provided formal peer review of the study and offered many constructive suggestions. At RAND, we thank Jayne Gordon and James Henderson for providing diligent and much valued assistance with a range of administrative tasks.

CHAPTER ONE

Introduction

Background and Purpose of This Study

The past two decades have been a time of intense change and upheaval in the California workers' compensation system. In the early 2000s, workers' compensation insurance premiums in the state were skyrocketing and the system was widely believed to be in crisis. This concern resulted in a sweeping reform effort in April 2004 that led to dramatic changes in the way that medical and indemnity benefits were delivered. One of the biggest changes made by the 2004 reform bill, referred to as Senate Bill (S.B.) 899, was to require disability ratings to be based upon the fifth edition of the American Medical Association's *Guides to the Evaluation of Permanent Impairment* (Cocchiarella and Andersson, 2001), referred to hereafter as AMA *Guides*. Previously, benefits had been determined by a unique California Permanent Disability Rating Schedule (PDRS), which critics had derided as subjective and inaccurate. After the adoption of these reforms, the average costs of workers' compensation claims fell for a short period and premiums fell for several years.

In the late 2000s, a pair of developments led to a push for further changes to the system. The first was that premiums began to rise once more, largely driven by rising costs associated with the provision of medical care for injured workers. The second was evidence that the 2004 reforms had led to a dramatic cut in permanent partial disability (PPD) benefits for disabled workers. The nature of the AMA *Guides* was such that disability ratings were significantly lower on average than the ratings under the pre–2005 PDRS. Because California PPD benefit levels are tied to disability ratings by law, disability benefits and replacement rates of lost income fell substantially after the reforms took effect (Seabury et al., 2011). Although large increases in PPD benefits were enacted in 2002 as part of Assembly Bill (A.B.) 749, the reductions in ratings and benefits observed after implementation of S.B. 899 raised concerns among stakeholders that S.B. 899 may have imposed a considerable burden on disabled workers. These concerns may have been colored by evidence that PPD benefits in earlier periods had been of questionable adequacy (Peterson et al., 1998).

In response to these controversies, California enacted S.B. 863 in September 2012. This bill had the dual goals of attempting to contain medical costs for injured workers while restoring some of the PPD benefits for permanently disabled workers reduced under S.B. 899. Consequently, the bill made many changes to permanent disability benefits. One of the new bill's most significant changes was to eliminate what was known as the future earnings capacity (FEC) variable, a scaling factor that adjusted AMA *Guides* ratings according to the type of injury.[1]

---

[1] Technically, S.B. 863 did not eliminate the FEC, it simply fixed it at 1.4 for all workers, whereas before the range was 1.1–1.4 with an average of 1.22 among single-impairment cases. (It is more complex to report an average FEC factor for multiple-impairment cases because the FEC is defined at the impairment level.)

Another important change was to raise the weekly benefit cap on PPD benefit levels, which had remained at the same level since 2006. The bill prohibited compensation based on certain controversial types of impairments that were secondary to the original impairment (e.g., sexual dysfunction or sleep disorder) and made various adjustments to administrative aspects of the system (such as the timing of permanent disability advances).

The reform created a return to work program to be funded at $120 million per year that would provide supplemental payments to injured workers whose permanent disability benefits are disproportionately low in comparison to their earnings losses. The bill provided the director of the Department of Industrial Relations (DIR) wide leeway in the design and implementation of the program, as discussed in an earlier RAND report (Seabury and Scherer, 2013) for the California Commission on Health and Safety and Workers' Compensation (CHSWC). Finally, the bill required CHSWC to conduct a study "to compare average loss of earnings for employees who sustained work-related injuries with permanent disability ratings under the schedule."

Evaluating the effect of S.B. 863 on benefit adequacy and equity poses several challenges. Typically, benefit adequacy is measured over an extended period of three to five years after the date of injury (Reville, Seabury, et al., 2005). However, this requires a substantial lag between the passage of a reform and the availability of data with which to analyze its effect. Prior RAND work for CHSWC addressed a similar issue to evaluate the 2004 reforms by simulating the predicted five-year losses of injured workers injured after the reforms. We adopt a similar approach in this case. However, in our analysis, we must deal with the fact that in 2008 the United States experienced the biggest economic slowdown since the Great Depression. The so-called Great Recession had a significant and lasting negative impact on the labor market, and potentially drove post-injury earnings and employment in ways that are not well understood.

To help CHSWC and other interested policymakers in understanding how S.B. 863 has and will affect outcomes for injured workers, we study the earnings of recent PPD beneficiaries in California. Specifically, we identify trends in earnings loss and employment for injured workers during the years 2005–2012 and estimate what fraction of losses was replaced by benefits over this time period. We then estimate what fraction would have been replaced had the changes of S.B. 863 been in place, and then project the likely future influence on replacement rates as the return to work program is implemented and economic conditions improve.

Research Questions

In order to understand how the post-injury experiences of permanently disabled workers in California have been affected by the Great Recession, and to evaluate the implications of the changes brought about by S.B. 863 for the adequacy of disability benefits, we address the following research questions:

- How have earnings losses and return to work associated with permanently disabling workplace injuries in California varied over the last decade?
- How much of the changes in earnings losses and return to work were driven by broader economic factors compared with changes in the characteristics of workers who filed claims?
- What is the effect of S.B. 863 on the adequacy of benefits?

- Will the S.B. 863 reforms affect the equity of benefits?
- To what extent do different aspects of the reforms account for changes in adequacy or equity?

Organization of This Report

In Chapter Two, we provide background on workers' compensation reform in California, and suggest a framework for evaluation. We also describe recent trends in the California economy that will be important for putting our evaluation in context. In Chapter Three, we describe the data and methods we use in our analysis. Chapter Four presents the results of our analysis of earnings losses and return to work for permanently disabled workers in California injured during the years 2005–2012. In particular, we spend considerable time evaluating how the Great Recession of the late 2000s affected outcomes for disabled workers. In Chapter Five, we assess how S.B. 863 affected the adequacy of disability benefits. We do this by estimating what replacement rates of lost income would have been for workers injured during the years 2005–2012 had S.B. 863 been in place over this entire period. Chapter Six details the effects of S.B. 863 on benefit equity. We finish with conclusions and policy recommendations. The appendixes contain information on methods and supplemental results.

CHAPTER TWO

Policy Background

This chapter provides some general background on the goals of workers' compensation policies and defines some criteria that we use to evaluate California's system. We then describe relevant features of California's workers' compensation system and detail the history of reform to permanent partial disability benefits in California. Finally, we provide some background on the disruption to labor markets caused by the Great Recession, which may affect outcomes for disabled workers.

Criteria for Evaluating Workers' Compensation Policies

State workers' compensation systems are designed to compensate workers for the medical costs and lost income they suffer as a result of work-related injuries or illnesses. Prior to the adoption of state workers' compensation systems in the early part of the twentieth century, compensation for work-related injuries and illnesses in the United States was provided through the tort system.[1] Based on civil tort law, workers injured on the job were entitled to full compensation for both economic and noneconomic damages suffered (potentially including punitive damages), but only when they could demonstrate that their injuries or illnesses resulted through negligence entirely on the part of employers. As is common in the tort system, actual recovery of damages was a costly and uncertain process. Workers' compensation was adopted as a compromise system that essentially carved out the compensation of workplace injuries from the tort system. Rather, workers' compensation would operate as a no-fault compensation system that offered full medical and partial income benefits to injured workers. These systems were seen as a compromise in which workers received benefits with greater certainty but only at reduced levels (Fishback and Kantor 1996).

Because workers' compensation benefits provide only partial compensation, there has historically been intense interest in monitoring the actual level of compensation they provide. Different standards have been used to evaluate these policies over time. The 1972 Report of the National Commission on State Workmen's Compensation Laws (the National Commission Report), probably the most comprehensive evaluation of the design of state workers' compensation programs, relied primarily on what is known as the *adequacy* and *equity* criteria to evaluate

---

[1] For a more detailed account of the history of workers' compensation, including a discussion of who benefited and who lost, see Fishback and Kantor (1996).

benefits. In addition, Berkowitz and Burton, Jr. (1987) suggest additional criteria based on the system's *affordability* and *efficiency*.[2] We define each of these in turn.

Adequacy

The adequacy of benefits is typically measured through the replacement rate of lost income. For temporary disability benefits, the standard for adequacy is generally held to be a replacement rate of two-thirds of lost pre-tax income or 80 percent of after-tax income (National Commission, 1972; National Academy of Social Insurance [NASI], 2004). For permanent disability benefits, there is less consensus about what the target replacement rate should be. The National Commission fell short of adopting the two-thirds statutory replacement rate as a standard, though later, in 2004, such a standard was recommended by a study panel of NASI. A complicating factor with permanent disability benefits is that they vary considerably depending on the timeline over which they are measured (Seabury et al., 2011). At the very least, a two-thirds threshold is a useful benchmark against which to compare replacement rates. Pre-tax rates that fall significantly below this level—and after-tax rates that fall significantly below 80 percent—are of potential concern.

Equity

The equity standard refers to the notion that workers who experience injuries and illnesses with similar severity should receive comparable levels of compensation. From the standpoint of income replacement, this means that workers with injuries of similar severity should have similar replacement rates. Based on how it has been applied in practice, the equity criterion does not necessarily require that workers receive the exact same dollar amounts in compensation. For instance, higher wage workers will tend to have greater dollar losses, which means that under an equitable system they would receive more benefits on average. Equity does not even require that replacement rates are the same. State systems routinely cap the total benefits at some fixed dollar value (usually tied to the state average weekly wage), which means that higher-wage workers will have lower replacement rates on average, which will decrease as their wages exceed the cap. Similarly, the presence of benefit floors means that, all else equal, the lowest-wage workers will receive the highest replacement rates.

Note that the estimated replacement rate of lost income is a useful tool for evaluating equity. That is, workers' compensation benefits are equitable if workers with the same expected losses have approximately the same replacement rate of lost income. This approach has been used by several previous RAND studies (Reville, Seabury, et al., 2005; Bhattacharya et al., 2010; Seabury and Scherer, 2013).

Affordability

The affordability criterion is fairly straightforward, and refers to the cost of the workers' compensation system. An affordable system is simply one that employers, workers, and the public can afford while still attaining minimum levels of adequacy (Reville, Seabury, et al., 2005). Note that the costs of the system refer to both the actual cost of the benefits as well as the cost of administering and delivering them. The administrative costs of workers' compensation

---

[2] Berkowitz and Burton, Jr. (1987) distinguished delivery system efficiency (i.e., administrative efficiency) from other types of efficiency, but we combine these under a single category for simplicity.

benefits in state systems have generally been considered quite high (Berkowitz and Burton, Jr., 1987; Sengupta, Baldwin, and Reno, 2014).[3]

There is an inherent and direct conflict between making a system more adequate and making it more affordable. Holding expected losses constant, we make workers' compensation benefits more adequate by increasing them, but this makes the system less affordable. There is some evidence that interventions that reduce expected losses, such as employer-based return to work programs, can serve the dual aim of making a system more affordable and more adequate (Seabury et al., 2011; McLaren, Reville, and Seabury, 2010). Additionally, improvements in administrative efficiency can lower the overhead cost of delivering benefits, which makes the system more affordable without hurting its adequacy.

Efficiency

Broadly defined, efficiency incorporates the indirect costs associated with workers' compensation benefits. This includes behavioral effects such as disincentives to return to work. So, a workers' compensation system is more efficient if it achieves a given level of adequacy without creating adverse work incentives. Efficiency can also incorporate factors such as administrative delay or the levels of disputes. Other factors such as incentives for injury prevention—by employers and workers—can also be included here. While not all of these are easily measured, the effect of any given reform proposal on the efficiency of benefits could represent a significant portion of the total social costs or benefits of the proposal.

In this report, we focus our attention on the adequacy and equity of benefits. However, it is important to keep in mind that these changes also influence the affordability and efficiency of the system. Focusing too much on any one aspect of the system could lead to changes that create imbalance and require further change to correct. Arguably, that describes some of the patterns of California's history of reforming the workers' compensation system.

Compensating Permanent Disabilities in California

As in other states, California's workers' compensation system requires employers to provide medical payments and cash indemnity benefits to workers who experience job-related injuries or illnesses.[4] California requires all employers, regardless of size, to have coverage for workers' compensation. To obtain coverage, employers may self-insure or purchase workers' compensation from a private insurance carrier or the State Compensation Insurance Fund. California employers wishing to self-insure must obtain certification from the DIR, and to do so they must be able to demonstrate sufficient financial resources. Another option for employers that are too small to meet the self-insured requirements is to combine efforts with other employers and self-insure as a private group or as a joint public authority.

Nonfatal workplace-related injuries or illnesses are classified as medical-only, temporary disability, or permanent disability. Medical-only claims involve no lost time, only medical treatment. A temporary work-related injury or illness is defined as one that prevents a worker from

---

[3] Although in some sense this is relative, as the administrative costs of the tort system are probably even higher (Studdert et al., 2006).

[4] Employers are also required to provide some death benefits to the dependents of workers who have died from a workplace injury or illness, though occupational fatalities are relatively infrequent.

doing his or her usual work for more than three days or the worker is hospitalized overnight.[5] Workers with a temporary condition will collect weekly total temporary disability (TTD) or temporary partial disability benefits until they return to work at full wage or reach maximum medical improvement (MMI). Injured workers who attain MMI but still have some residual disability as a result of the injury are potentially eligible for PPD benefits.

Historically, the California approach to compensating permanent disabilities has differed considerably from that of most states. The rating system in California has been the center of considerable controversy, including numerous allegations that it is overly subjective and promotes disputes (Berkowitz and Burton, Jr., 1987; Reville, Seabury, et al., 2005). For a detailed description of the system and its development over time, see Reville, Seabury, et al. (2005) and Seabury et al. (2011). Below, we discuss how reforms to the system in 2004 led to the adoption of a system based on the AMA *Guides*. The implementation of this change resulted in a substantial decline in benefits and helped motivate the adoption of S.B. 863.

Workers' Compensation Reform in California

The compensation of permanent partial disabilities has been at the heart of many controversies involving the California workers' compensation system over the years. Several past studies by RAND conducted for CHSWC have questioned the adequacy of California's PPD benefit levels (Peterson et al., 1998; Reville and Schoeni, 2001; Reville, Schoeni, and Martin, 2002; Seabury et al., 2011). This is despite the fact that on a statutory basis, the benefits in California are not noticeably lower than in other states (Reville, Seabury, et al., 2005). Nonetheless, concerns about adequacy have motivated several reforms to benefit levels over the years, including S.B. 863.

In California, the weekly benefit cap for TTD benefits was fixed at $490 per week from 1996 to 2002, when it was raised in several steps for injuries occurring on or after January 1, 2004, by A.B. 749 and tied to a cost of living adjustment based on the state average weekly wage after 2006 (the weekly maximum for injuries occurring in 2015 is $1,103.29). Prior to April 19, 2004 (the date of adoption of S.B. 899), workers received TTD benefits until they reached MMI or were medically cleared to return to work. After April 19, 2004, however, TTD benefits were capped at 104 weeks except for some claims involving more severe injuries. Workers with these types of injuries—examples include amputations or severe burns—receive TTD benefits for up to 240 weeks (Labor Code §4656[c][2]).

The amount of PPD benefits received by the injured worker is tied directly to the disability rating. The maximum weekly benefit is two-thirds of wages subject to a weekly cap that increased with the disability rating; for example, workers injured on January 1, 2006, after A.B. 749 was fully implemented, would have been eligible for up to $230 per week if their disability ratings were under 70 percent, and up to $270 per week if their disability ratings were 70 percent to 99 percent. Also, the number of weeks for which benefits are available is an increasing function of the disability rating. Finally, workers with a rating of 70 or more are eligible for a small weekly life pension.

---

[5]   If an injury or illness requires the worker to be out of work for 14 days or longer, the first three days are covered retroactively.

The passage of S.B. 899 in 2004 led to substantial changes in the disability rating system with adoption of the system based on the AMA *Guides* (Labor Code §4660[b][1]). The new rating system abandoned the old subjective factors and work capacity guidelines, although it did keep the age and occupation modifiers. Additionally, S.B. 899 required the administrative director to incorporate empirical data on earnings losses for disabled workers to adjust disability ratings, which was done through what were referred to as FEC adjustments. The FEC adjustments ranked different disabilities based on the estimates of earnings losses reported in Seabury, Reville, and Neuhauser (2004). There were eight categories, or "ranks," numbered one to eight. Higher categories receive larger upward adjustments to their disability ratings. The adjustments range from a 10-percent increase for the first category up to a 40-percent increase for the eighth category.

Another change in the disability rating system introduced by S.B. 899 was the introduction of new rules on how responsibility for the disability is split between the employer and worker ("apportionment"). S.B. 899 repealed the previous rules on apportionment and added this new requirement:

> A physician shall make an apportionment determination by finding what approximate percentage of the permanent disability was caused by the direct result of injury arising out of and occurring in the course of employment and what approximate percentage of the permanent disability was caused by other factors both before and subsequent to the industrial injury, including prior industrial injuries. (Labor Code §§4663 [c])

Furthermore, Labor Code §4664 (a) states, "The employer shall only be liable for the percentage of permanent disability directly caused by the injury arising out of and occurring in the course of employment." Put more simply, the new apportionment rules reduce permanent disability ratings by the fraction of disability that the physician deems was not work related.

The net effect of the changes to the permanent disability rating system brought about by S.B. 899 was a substantial reduction in the size of permanent disability ratings. The adoption of the AMA *Guides* led to a reduction because the average rating in the AMA *Guides* is lower than the rating assigned to a similar impairment evaluated using the pre–2005 PDRS. Neuhauser (2007) found that the average permanent disability rating in California after adoption of the AMA *Guides* system was 41.7 percent lower than under the PDRS prior to adoption. Additionally, he found that 9.8 percent of all permanent disability cases included apportionment in 2006, leading to an average reduction in ratings of 40.1 percent in apportioned cases. Overall, the apportioning of permanent disability to causation reduced total permanent partial disability benefit payments by almost 6 percent, and the total decline in permanent disability awards that could be attributed to lower disability ratings was more than 50 percent.

In addition to the above changes, S.B. 899 also introduced a two-tier PPD benefit. The provision, commonly referred to as bump up/bump down, specifies that employees are entitled to a 15-percent increase in their disability benefits if they are not offered a return to regular, modified, or alternative work, and a 15-percent decrease in benefits if they are. The 30-percent swing in disability benefits potentially provides a strong incentive for employers to make a return to work offer for injured workers. To be eligible for the bump down, the employer must make the qualified work offer within 60 days of the injury being declared permanent and stationary (P&S). The bump up/bump down also had the important policy objective of better targeting PPD benefits at those with higher post-injury wage loss. Workers that return to the at-injury employer have substantially lower long-term wage loss than those who do not.

While the tiered benefit program provides unambiguous incentives to bring injured workers back to work and better targeting of benefits, implementation problems limited its effectiveness. One of the chief limitations had to do with the timing. In order to be eligible for the bump down, an employer has to make a qualified offer within 60 days of P&S date, but an employer (or insurer) may have been paying PPD benefits long before the P&S date was reached. In California, workers become eligible for PPD benefits two weeks after TTD benefit payments end, even if the injured worker has not yet reached MMI (§4650[b]). If a worker later settles the value of the permanent disability benefits, these advance payments are deducted from the final settlement amount. The reason this affected the usefulness of the tiered benefit is that PPD advancements are made at a statutory rate before any adjustment (i.e., before the bump up or bump down is applied). In many cases, even the majority of cases, it can be six months or more between the date at which an injured worker is cleared to return to work (meaning PPD benefits will often start well before the P&S date). For a worker with a disability rating of 11 (the mean rating in the California Disability Evaluation Unit [DEU] for unrepresented claims in the new schedule) the full PPD award could be paid out before the post-P&S period is reached. Given the advancement at statutory levels, it is unclear that the bump down was used frequently enough to have a significant effect on return to work.

In the late 2000s, two developments increased pressure for further reform. The first was that premiums began to rise once more, largely driven by rising costs associated with the provision of medical care for injured workers. The second was a growing body of evidence that the 2004 reforms had led to a dramatic cut in PPD benefits for disabled workers. Even after the FEC adjustments, disability ratings (and thus disability benefit levels) were significantly lower on average than the ratings under the old schedule, and replacement rates of lost income fell by 26 percent after the reforms (Seabury et al., 2011). Given past evidence showing that California already had questionable benefit adequacy under the old benefit levels (Peterson et al., 1998), there was concern that, despite the large increase in benefits under A.B. 749, the effort to cut costs had imposed considerable burden on injured and disabled workers.

In September 2012, California adopted S.B. 863 as an attempt to contain medical costs for injured workers while restoring some of the PPD benefits that had been reduced. The bill made many changes to permanent disability benefits, including elimination of the FEC variable (replaced with a fixed multiplier of 1.4), an increase in the amount of wages that can be considered for calculation of PPD benefits, a limitation on compensation based on certain controversial types of add-on impairments (e.g., sexual dysfunction, psychological disorders, and sleep disorders), and various adjustments to administrative aspects of the system (such as the timing of PD advances). The reform also created a return to work program to be funded at $120 million per year that would provide supplemental payments to injured workers whose permanent disability benefits are disproportionately low in comparison to their earnings losses. The bill provided the director of the DIR wide leeway in the design and implementation of the program. In addition, the bill required the director and CHSWC to determine eligibility and the amount of payments to be made based on a study.

California's Labor Market Since 2005

The adequacy of workers' compensation benefits fundamentally depends on the severity of earnings and employment losses caused by occupational injury and illness. Because earnings

differences in outcomes between workers with disability and those without. While both groups suffered significant declines in labor force participation and employment rates between 2006 and 2010, evidence points to weaker recovery for the disabled workers: the unemployment rate among workers without disability rose from 4.6 percent in March 2006 to 10.0 percent in 2010 and then fell to 8.2 percent in 2012, whereas the rate among those with disabilities rose from 12.6 percent in March 2006 to 18.3 percent in the same month of 2010 and had climbed another 2.7 percentage points two years later (Livermore and Honeycutt, 2015).

The BLS data make it clear that the dramatic changes in economic and labor force conditions during the Great Recession had substantial negative impacts on the employment of all workers. However, workers experiencing new occupational disabilities during a downturn may face a very different constellation of factors affecting retention of employment. On the one hand, special protections for workers experiencing occupational injuries, built into the Labor Code and case law, may mitigate the effect of a recession. On the other hand, if occupational injuries lead to more frequent job separations, injured workers may be especially vulnerable to post-injury job loss with associated negative impacts on future long-term income. Very little research has addressed the influence of the business cycle on outcomes for injured workers. A major focus of this report is to address this gap so that the effect of S.B. 863 can be evaluated with the greatest possible accuracy.

CHAPTER THREE

Methods

The policy questions posed in this report center on earnings losses, impairment ratings, and benefits among permanently disabled workers. We measure these outcomes by analyzing administrative data from several state agencies. This chapter describes the methods we use to measure earnings losses and provides an overview of our data sources. We measure economic outcomes using the matching methodology used in numerous prior RAND studies for CHSWC, including Peterson et al. (1998); Reville, Boden, et al. (2001); Reville and Schoeni (2001); Reville, Schoeni, and Martin (2002); Reville, Seabury, et al. (2005); and Seabury et al. (2011). We also illustrate our method by providing estimates of the negative impact of injury on earnings and employment for the average worker injured during the years 2005–2012.

Measuring Losses from Injury

We describe the empirical challenge to estimating earnings losses using Figure 3.1, which illustrates the hypothetical losses from a permanently disabling workplace injury. The dashed line represents the "potential" earnings a worker would have in the absence of an injury. Potential earnings increase over time, representing the increased earnings associated with increasing experience in the labor market or increasing tenure at the employer. The solid line represents the actual earnings of the injured worker. At the time of injury, the worker receives no earnings for some time while recovering from the injury. This is the period during which workers' compensation temporary disability benefits are received.

At some point, the worker returns to work, perhaps in some modified capacity. In the example in the figure, the worker returns at lower earnings than prior to injury. The worker recovers earnings over time, as the wages converge closer to what they would have been absent the injury. In this example, at the end of the observed period the worker makes more than he or she made prior to the injury, but not as much as he or she would have made if he or she had not been injured.

The shaded area in the figure represents the total lost earnings over the period after the injury. Estimating the size of this area and determining what fraction is replaced by workers' compensation benefits are the goals of this analysis. Whereas wages received while the claimant is injured are readily observable (the solid line in Figure 3.1), the challenge in estimating earning losses lies in estimating what the workers would have earned if uninjured, represented by the dotted line.

This example illustrates the metrics we can use to estimate the negative economic impact of a disability. The shaded area in Figure 3.1 represents the total earnings lost as a result of the

Figure 3.1
Hypothetical Effect on Earnings after a Workplace Injury

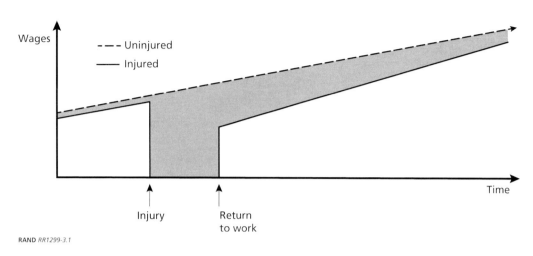

RAND *RR1299-3.1*

disability. To measure the length of time out of work, we can measure whether the employee has returned at different points after injury, i.e., measuring the point of return to work. Whether we evaluate the effect on the actual dollars earned or the time out of work, both represent adverse outcomes for injured workers.

Administrative Data Sources for Studying Earnings Losses

Our data in this study are similar to the data used in past studies (e.g., Peterson et al., 1998; Reville, Seabury, et al., 2005). Workers' compensation claims data are linked to earnings data for the claimant based on their Social Security number (SSN), and this information is combined with earnings data to identify the control group. We use data on workers' compensation claimants from two sources: the Workers' Compensation Information System (WCIS) and the DEU.

WCIS Data on Claims

The WCIS, which was developed and is managed by the DIR, was legislated in 1993 and implemented starting in 2001. Information at the individual claim level is transferred from claims administrators to DIR using the Electronic Data Interchange (EDI) formats developed by the International Association of Industrial Accident Boards and Commissions. In 2001, DIR began collecting EDI versions of the First Report of Injury (FROI), which includes detailed information on the injured worker, employer, nature of the injury, and event leading to injury. Subsequent Report of Injury (SROI) data are also included and are transaction-level data on indemnity payments, lost time, and the timing of important events on a claim such as return to work and claim closure. In 2007, DIR began collecting transaction-level medical treatment data at the claim level, including procedures, diagnoses, and payments. In addition, claims administrators are required to report at least annually on individual claim-level data on benefits paid to date, including both medical payments and indemnity payments by type of indemnity.

These data represent an important source of information for analyzing and evaluating the California workers' compensation system. However, there are a number of limitations. Most important, while improving over time, these data are incomplete with a substantial (but unknown) fraction of claims administrators not reporting any information beyond the FROI. Consequently, the WCIS may not be representative of the system as a whole and the representativeness and composition may change over time. Again, reporting has been improving over time due to efforts by DIR: recent statutory changes authorizing financial penalties for noncompliance are expected to increase participation, and technical difficulties that interfered with data submission have been addressed in recent years.

One additional concern regarding the WCIS is that data quality is likely to vary across data elements. In some cases, problems arise because claims administrators have discretion in reporting that makes it inadvisable to take the information in WCIS at face value. In our study, this concern is most serious with respect to detailed information about the type and severity of permanent impairments reported to the WCIS. The "permanent impairment percentage" referred to in the instruction manual for claims administrators could reasonably be construed to mean the standard rating associated with an impairment, the final rating before apportionment (after adjustments for future earnings capacity, occupation, and age), or the final rating after apportionment. A related concern is that permanent disability information (the impairment type, rating percent, and incurred indemnity amounts) may be estimated early in the life of a claim for initial reporting and insurance reserving purposes, but may not be updated to reflect a worker's actual impairment rating. We treat permanent disability information in the WCIS as a noisy measure of impairment severity but never take it at face value to calculate statutory benefits or identify PPD beneficiaries.

Furthermore, like most administrative systems, data elements that are not critical to administration on the claim can be subject to inconsistent and inaccurate reporting. For example, paid amounts will generally be accurate because they track important administrative information and are mandatory data elements on the relevant reports, but other details that would be valuable for our analysis, such as the date when the claimant obtained legal representation, may not be reliably or accurately reported because they are not required data elements in the EDI system underlying WCIS.

While these limitations mean that WCIS data has to be analyzed with care, the WCIS remains an extremely valuable resource. It may be most useful to consider the WCIS as representative of paid data for the private sector, since there are considerable gaps in local government reporting. Beyond that limitation, and if care is taken to limit some analyses to a subset of higher-quality reporting entities, information on the cost of claims, duration of disability, medical treatment patterns, and costs and trends in all cost components over time can be reliably estimated.

The Division of Workers' Compensation (DWC) within the California Department of Industrial Relations extracted all FROI and SROI data in the WCIS for cases with dates of injury in 2005 or later. The data were current as of September 2014. DWC provided us with a de-identified file containing selected data elements from these records.

Disability Evaluation Unit Data on Ratings

Disability ratings determine the level of statutory permanent partial disability benefits in California. The permanent disability rating is a number between 0 percent and 100 percent that indicates the severity of permanent disability, with higher numbers indicating greater severity and leading to larger amounts of indemnity payments for permanent partial disability. While disability ratings are critically important for determining the level of indemnity payments for permanent partial disability, they do not affect a worker's access to compensation for medical care. It is worth noting that, for injuries occurring between 2004 and 2012, the permanent disability rating did affect the value of the Supplemental Job Displacement Benefit (SJDB). The SJDB, which is a voucher for educational and vocational rehabilitation services available to workers who do not receive a qualifying offer to return to work at the at-injury employer, ranged in value from $4,000 for low permanent disability ratings (below 15 percent) to $10,000 for the most severe ratings (50 percent or higher) (Labor Code Sec. 4658.5). S.B. 863 set the value of the SJDB to a constant $6,000 regardless of disability ratings for injuries in 2013 or later years, so the permanent disability rating no longer affects access to vocational rehabilitation (Labor Code Sec. 4658.7). Earnings loss estimates in our study should be interpreted in the context of the SJDB, meaning that access to vocational rehabilitation was somewhat higher for workers with higher permanent disability (PD) ratings.[1]

When a worker's impairment has reached *maximum medical improvement*, meaning that "his or her condition is well stabilized and unlikely to change substantially in the next year with or without medical treatment," a physician can evaluate the severity of the impairment and produce an impairment rating for each distinct impairment that may lead to a loss of earnings capacity lasting beyond the date of maximum medical improvement (Division of Workers' Compensation, 2005). Disability ratings are assigned according to procedures outlined in the PDRS issued by DWC, which specifies rules for combining multiple impairments and calculating *final* ratings (which are used to determine benefits) from the *standard* ratings assigned to a worker's specific impairments.

As discussed above, the WCIS is not a reliable source for detailed information about PD ratings. In order to get a sample of claims with more reliable data on ratings and precision on the type of impairment, we use data from the DEU. The DEU reviews medical reports to produce a disability rating.

The DEU ratings include precise data on

- type of physician evaluating the worker (treating physician, qualified medical evaluator [QME], or agreed medical evaluator [AME])
- whether the case is represented
- impairment(s)
- percent impairment for each impairment
- effect of occupational adjustment
- effect of age adjustment
- effect of apportionment, if any.

From the DEU, we received transaction data for claims rated between 2005 and May 2015. The DEU performed an average of 90,000 ratings on approximately 60,000 unique claims each year. In the early years, the ratings were primarily for claims rated under the pre–2005 PDRS. In the later years, 95 percent of ratings are under the AMA-based rating schedule. For this

---

[1]   SJDB eligibility and payments are not consistently reported in our WCIS data, and we do not include SJDB payments in our estimates of statutory benefits. We note that the range of SJDB payment amounts ($4,000 to $10,000) in place for the period 2004–2012 is very small compared to the range of statutory benefits.

study, we excluded claims rated under the pre–2005 PDRS, concentrating solely on ratings under the AMA-based schedule. Each DEU rating follows a specific format, dictated by the AMA *Guides* and the California PDRS. The standardization of this format allowed us to parse the ratings data (which are entered as text) and, with some data cleaning, construct an analytic dataset capturing each step in the disability rating process.

Each impairment evaluated by the evaluating physician is identified by an impairment number, which is listed in the PDRS and corresponds to the chapter and section in the AMA *Guides*. A rating in units of *Whole Person Impairment* (WPI) is assigned by the DEU rater based on the impairment number and the description supplied by the doctor. Each impairment number has an associated FEC factor. The product of the WPI and the FEC gives the standard rating after adjustment for FEC. Under S.B. 899, the FEC ranged from 1.1 to 1.4, depending on the impairment. Under S.B. 863, the FEC takes a single value, 1.4.

Next the rater assigns the worker to one of 43 occupational groups based on a description of the worker's primary job at injury. Each occupation group-impairment number pair is associated with an occupational factor, a letter from *C* to *J*, based on how the impairment is thought to interact with the occupational demands of the worker's job to affect future earnings. The effect of the occupational adjustment depends on the letter and the FEC-adjusted standard rating. As an example, an FEC-adjusted standard rating of 10 percent with a *C* occupational adjustment (the lowest factor) would be reduced to 7 percent while the same rating with a *J* adjustment (the highest factor) would be increased to 16 percent.

The DEU rater then adjusts the rating for age. Ratings are reduced for workers younger than 37 and increased for workers older than 42. The younger or older the worker, the larger the magnitude of the adjustment. Again assuming a 10-percent rating after occupational adjustment, a 21-year-old worker would have the rating reduced to 8 percent and a 62-year-old worker would be increased to 13 percent. The age-adjusted rating is the final rating before apportionment, if any.

The doctor's report is required to indicate whether any of the final disability rating should be apportioned to non-industrial cause, reducing the rating. Apportionment is not consistently observed for all DEU ratings. If the worker is unrepresented, the rating reliably indicates if apportionment should be applied (as reviewed by a workers' compensation administrative law judge) and the percent of cause that is industrial. However, if the worker is represented, apportionment is calculated only if the parties request it, and the data do not reflect any decision on whether the doctor's finding meets the legal standards required under statute and case law.

Each doctor's report can evaluate one or more impairments for each worker. Of cases evaluated under S.B. 899, 65.4 percent of workers have a single impairment evaluated, 19.3 percent have two impairments, and 15.3 percent have three or more impairments evaluated.

Each unique claim in the DEU data can have more than one doctor's report. This led to several situations that required decisions on how to determine the final disability rating.

- A doctor can submit an updated evaluation on a claim where the impairment has evolved. In this case we chose the latest report, chronologically.
- A second report can be written by a specialist covering a separate impairment. In this case we combined the two reports using the rules for combining disabilities under the AMA *Guides*.

- A second, comprehensive report by a different physician (most commonly an AME), subsequent to an initial treating physician or QME report, could be submitted when agreed to by the parties. We used the latest report, chronologically.

A single doctor's report can also be rated more than once. This occurs when one or both parties request a rating under the AMA *Guides* and a rating based on the case law standard established by the *Almaraz* en banc decision by the Workers' Compensation Appeals Board (WCAB). When there was both an AMA *Guides* and *Almaraz* rating, we used the AMA *Guides* for the primary analyses presented here.[2] The implications of the *Alamaraz* decision are potentially important for the disability rating system, however, and we discuss them at length in Chapter Five of this report.

Some doctors' reports rated 0 percent under the AMA *Guides*, before apportionment. These were excluded from most analyses. We explicitly state when claims rating 0 percent under the AMA *Guides* are included. Finally, some reports were considered "not ratable" by the DEU because the reports were incomplete or the worker was not yet P&S. These reports were also excluded from analyses.

Roles of WCIS and DEU Data in This Study

The WCIS and the DEU have complementary strengths and weaknesses, so we rely on them to address different aspects of our research questions.

In this study, we treat the WCIS as our primary data source for estimating trends in earnings losses among PPD claimants in Chapter Four. Estimation of trends in outcomes through recent injuries is a major objective of this report, but differences in the timing of data capture in the WCIS and the DEU lead to substantially greater data lags between the injury date and the appearance of a case in the DEU. Figure 3.2 illustrates these differences using a stylized flowchart of a worker's progression from injury to recovery and permanent impairment (in the left-hand column) and the timing of data capture in the WCIS and the DEU. Workers with a high probability of permanent disability can be identified in the WCIS by the receipt of PPD benefit payments, which must be reported to the WCIS within 14 days after benefit payments begin.[3] In contrast, workers' evaluating physician reports can take months or even more than a year after reaching maximum medical improvement to reach the DEU, which makes it difficult to examine trends for recently injured workers using the DEU. The majority of the lag between injury and DEU evaluation is likely driven by the duration to maximum medical improvement (and is inherent in the disability process, since permanent impairment cannot be assessed before maximum medical improvement has been reached). However, additional administrative frictions (such as scheduling a QME examination, submission of a

---

[2]   Among reports rated between 2013 and 2015 by the DEU, 20 percent of reports on unrepresented cases and 25 percent of reports on represented cases included both an AMA rating and an alternative rating under *Almaraz*. When the DEU calculates an *Almaraz* rating, the rater almost always calculates the AMA *Guides* rating as well.

[3]   Payment of advance PPD benefits before a worker has reached maximum medical improvement may lead us to erroneously include in our sample some workers who are later determined not to qualify for PPD benefits. Unfortunately, we found that other data elements that might be used to confirm permanent disability (such as data on the impairment number or the PD rating) are frequently missing in the WCIS. When we examined cases with both DEU and WCIS data, we found that the cases that were missing these other data elements were no less severe on average than cases with complete data on PD ratings in the WCIS. We conclude that PPD benefit payments are our best option for identifying permanently disabled workers in the WCIS.

Using Matched Uninjured Coworkers as a Control Group

We estimate uninjured earnings in the post-injury period using the earnings of a matched comparison (control) group. The comparison group is made up of workers similar to the injured workers in the pre-injury period, but who did not experience a workplace injury during the time period under examination.

For each injured worker, we selected up to five workers employed at the same firm at the time of injury who had earnings close to the injured worker's over the year prior to injury. We define "close" as being within a band equal to the log earnings of the injured worker plus or minus 20 percent of the standard deviation of the log earnings of all injured workers. The comparison workers were also required to have similar tenure at the at-injury employer prior to the quarter of injury, where tenure is measured using three levels: less than or equal to one year on the job, one to two years, or more than two years. If more than five comparison workers met the matching criteria, we selected the five workers with the smallest difference in wages from the injured workers (ties were decided randomly). We sampled with replacement, meaning the same comparison workers could match to more than one injured worker. If a worker was injured in a later year, however, they were not allowed to be a comparison worker.

Here we describe formally how we use the matched data to estimate earnings losses. Let y_t^I represent the injured worker's earnings (where I denotes "injured" and the subscript t denotes "time from the injury"). Let y_t^U represent the comparison worker's earnings (where U denotes "uninjured"). We estimated y_t^U using the average earnings of the n comparison workers for that individual injured worker, where n is between 1 and 5, depending upon the number of available comparable uninjured workers at the injured worker's employer. For any injured worker, the undiscounted earnings loss between the time of injury, which we denoted as $t = 0$, and some future date, T, is defined as follows:

$$\text{earnings loss} = \sum_{t=0}^{T} (y_t^U - y_t^I)$$

Usually, when we report earnings losses we report the average of this quantity across all injured workers.

In some sense, return to work is easy to measure: we simply observe whether or not an individual is working (and at what point) after an injury occurs. In some cases, however, injured workers may exit the labor force for reasons totally independent of their disability. Simply asking whether or not disabled workers are working in the post-injury period ignores the possibility that they may not have worked even in the absence of a disability. Thus, to estimate the negative impact of injuries on return to work it is necessary to compare the likelihood that disabled workers are working in the post-injury period compared to the likelihood that uninjured "control" workers are working.

We can formally define our return to work estimates as follows. Let h_t^I be a variable that equals 1 if earnings are reported by an injured worker in quarter t (i.e., if $y_t^I > 0$), and let h_t^U be a similar indicator for uninjured workers (we focus on quarters because the data we propose to use is quarterly earnings data). If a person has earnings reported in that quarter, then we presume he or she is working in that quarter. Furthermore, let $Pr(h_t^I)$ and $Pr(h_t^U)$ denote the probability that injured and uninjured workers report positive earnings in quarter t. In general, we do not observe the probability that an individual works but simply observe whether or not

Table 3.1
Control Worker Match Rate by Size of At-Injury Employer

Number of Employees	Percentage Matching at Least 1 Control	
	WCIS	DEU
1–10	23.2	19.3
11–50	62.0	54.1
50–100	81.6	73.3
101–500	92.7	86.1
501–1,000	97.4	92.0
1,001–5,000	98.8	94.3
Over 5,000	99.4	94.8
Overall Match Rate	88.9	78.1
Number of Injured Workers with a Matched Control	357,212	185,031

NOTES: The table reports the fraction of workers with at least one valid matched control by employer size. The denominator used to calculate these match rates is the population of workers' compensation claims that were matched to a valid wage history. For the WCIS, we restricted attention in this calculation to workers injured in 2005–2012 with paid PPD indemnity benefits.

he or she works. However, aggregating to the fraction of individuals who work provides us with an estimate of the probability that an individual works. We can thus define return to work in a given quarter as

$$\text{relative employment}_t = \frac{Pr(h_t^I)}{Pr(h_t^U)}.$$

In some cases, we might ask whether or not an individual returns to the at-injury employer. Return to the at-injury employer can be examined in a similar fashion, with the h_t variables only equaling 1 if the injured worker reports earnings from the at-injury employer.

One limitation of this matching procedure is that it is more difficult to match individuals in smaller firms, thus we are unable to estimate losses for many of these workers. Table 3.1 reports the match rate for both the WCIS and DEU samples. The match rate in the WCIS is lowest for small firms and climbs steadily to reach 99 percent at the largest employers. Because employer size may be an important predictor of post-injury outcomes, we apply a weighting methodology used in previous RAND studies to correct our estimates for match failure.[5] The corrected estimates are valid for the total population of cases appearing in WCIS, not just those with a matched control worker.

---

[5]   See Bhattacharya et al. (2010) for a full description of this method.

Table 3.2
Earnings, Employment, and Return to Work over the First Three Post-Injury Years

Characteristic	First Post-Injury Year (%)	Second Post-Injury Year (%)	Third Post-Injury Year (%)
Relative earnings	69	70	71
Relative employment	73	74	76
Relative at-injury employment	70	63	58

NOTES: Earnings, employment, and return to work over first three post-injury years relative to controls. Weights used to correct for match failure. WCIS injured workers receiving PPD benefits 2005–2012, unweighted N = 345,282. Third-year outcomes available only for 2005–2011, unweighted N = 320,770.

in WCIS with an injury date between 2005 and 2012. Relative earnings in the first post-injury year were 69 percent of control worker earnings, meaning that permanently disabled workers earned 31 percent less on average than they would have if they had remained uninjured. Relative earnings recover slightly through the second and third post-injury years, reaching 70 percent of control worker earnings in the second year and 71 percent in the third year.

Similarly, we measure employment for injured workers relative to control workers at the end of the first, second, and third post-injury years (i.e., in the fourth, eighth, and twelfth post-injury quarters).[9] The fourth and eighth post-injury quarters are indicated by vertical lines on Figure 3.4. The second row of Table 3.2, which reports relative employment for the average injured worker in the WCIS, indicates that injured workers are 73 percent as likely as control workers to be employed in both the fourth and the eighth post-injury quarters. Similar to the dynamics of earnings shown in Figure 3.3, relative employment recovers slightly in the third post-injury year and reaches 76 percent of control worker employment in the twelfth post-injury quarter. This improvement in relative employment, however, is driven by the fact that control worker employment declines faster than injured worker employment rather than by an increase in the level of employment among injured workers.

A third outcome measure that we examine is employment at the at-injury employer, defined by receipt of any wages from the at-injury employer. Figure 3.5 shows injured and control worker time profiles for at-injury employment. Compared to overall employment, which stabilized and began to increase slightly by two years post-injury, relative at-injury employment continues to decline steadily throughout the first two post-injury years. The third row of Table 3.2 reports that relative at-injury employment falls from 70 percent in the fourth post-injury quarter to 63 percent in the eighth post-injury quarter and then to 58 percent in the twelfth post-injury quarter.

Discussion

The evidence presented in this chapter is meant to familiarize the reader with the magnitude of earnings and employment losses due to permanent disability and to illustrate how our outcome measures are defined. With consistently defined outcome measures, we can begin to analyze differences in earnings and employment losses both between workers at a point in time and

---

[9] We classify workers as employed if they have total wages from all employers in a quarter of $200 or more.

across cohorts of workers injured at different points in time. Of particular interest for this study are the effects of worker characteristics (such as age and gender), employer characteristics, and the type and severity of permanent impairment on earnings loss.

Although this report does not place a heavy emphasis on the relationship between job transitions, earnings losses, and long-term employment outcomes, Table 3.2 and Figure 3.3 highlighted some interesting differences in the dynamics of earnings, employment, and at-injury employment. The slow, sustained decline in relative at-injury employment is particularly interesting insofar as it suggests that injured workers may be at higher risk of job separations following an initial period of recovery. The distinction between initial return to work and successful return to work and the importance of post-injury job separations have been highlighted by other researchers (Butler, Johnson, and Baldwin, 1995; Boden and Galizzi, 2003).

The fact that relative employment recovers slightly over time suggests that at least some injured workers who separate from the at-injury employer are able to adapt to their impairments by changing jobs. However, the fact that the uptick in relative employment is not accompanied by higher relative earnings implies that some combination of lower wages and reduced hours among those injured workers who remain employed offsets any recovery in relative employment. While it is beyond the scope of this report, more careful study of the career paths of permanently disabled workers, perhaps with survey datasets that capture hours worked, could help shed light on the relative importance of wages and hours in post-injury earnings and begin to provide an evidence base that could help policymakers to mitigate earnings losses among permanently disabled workers more effectively.

We report outcomes over the first through third post-injury years in the body of this report to provide some insight into the dynamics of injured worker outcomes, but we focus primarily on earnings and employment during the second post-injury year. This choice is driven by data availability: the most recent available wage data at the time this report was prepared covered earnings through the end of 2014, so the most long-term outcome measure that can be consistently defined for all workers injured while S.B. 899 was in place is relative earnings in the second post-injury year.

The second post-injury year is somewhat earlier than might be ideal for evaluating the consequences of permanent disability, since many permanently disabled workers are likely to be on temporary total disability for at least a portion of this time window. This is problematic for several reasons. Conceptually, one might argue that earnings losses experienced during the total disability period should be excluded from consideration when assessing the adequacy and equity of permanent partial disability benefits: TTD benefits are paid during this time period, so PPD benefits understate the level of compensation provided by the workers' compensation system. Similarly, workers who have not reached maximum medical improvement by the start of the second post-injury year also may not have seen their earnings and employment outcomes stabilize sufficiently to capture their likely long-term outcomes. For example, workers who remain employed two years after injury have limited earnings losses relative to control workers in the long run, but still experience meaningful earnings losses in the immediate post-injury period before recovering. Notwithstanding these limitations, we find that a worker's relative earnings in the second post-injury year (which implicitly captures the effect of changes in employment and return to work at the at-injury employer) are reasonably predictive of longer-term earnings losses.

To evaluate the potential for bias due to our focus on a short follow-up period, we examined long-term earnings profiles for workers injured in 2008 or earlier, for whom we obtained five or more years of post-injury data. These data, which we present in Appendix A, show that injured and control worker earnings profiles are very close to parallel after the second post-injury year. For earnings and employment, relative outcomes in the second post-injury year may be a reasonable proxy for long-term relative outcomes. Relative at-injury firm employment continues to decline steadily through the fifth post-injury year.

The data assembled for this report represent the best available evidence on disability ratings and the economic consequences of workplace injury for the population of injured workers who receive PPD benefits in California. No data source is perfect, however, and it is worth noting certain limitations inherent in the use of administrative data. Income sources other than labor earnings and workers' compensation benefits are not captured in our data, so it is important to bear in mind that our earnings loss estimates may not accurately capture *income loss* if disabled workers become more likely to obtain income from sources other than wage employment (including self-employment, pensions, Social Security retirement, or other forms of disability insurance). As in most administrative data sources, we do not observe workers' ethnicity, citizenship status, and English-language fluency, characteristics that may be correlated with economic vulnerability and workers' ability to navigate the workers' compensation system.

Finally, readers should be aware that the population of interest in our study consists of injured workers who file workers' compensation claims. Many workers who experience occupational injury and illness never file workers' compensation claims, and the decision to file a claim is certain to be related to worker, employer, and injury characteristics in systematic and potentially complex ways (Azaroff, Levenstein, and Wegman, 2002). We simply cannot observe these injuries in workers' compensation claims data. Since the objective of this study is to evaluate workers' compensation policy, we do not view this as in any way a threat to the validity of our study. Rather, we mention this limitation in order to remind readers that they should exercise caution in extrapolating our findings regarding earnings losses to the wider population of workers who experience occupational injury or illness.

Another interesting feature of Figure 4.5 is that the drop in relative earnings in most industries is somewhat smaller than the economy-wide drop reported in Table 4.1. While this may seem surprising, it suggests that part of the overall trend may have been a change in the composition of the injured worker population. We accordingly investigate the influence of changes in industry mix and other compositional factors on the pattern of earnings losses over 2005–2012.[4]

Changes in the Composition of the Permanently Disabled Worker Population

The time profiles reported in Figures 4.1–4.4 and Table 4.1 indicate that outcomes for the average worker injured during the recession (2008–2009) and the recovery (2010–2012) were worse than outcomes for the average worker injured prior to the recession (2005–2007). The timing of these changes in outcomes suggests that labor market conditions were responsible for the deterioration of injured workers' economic outcomes. The evidence presented so far does not, however, prove that this is the case, as a number of alternative explanations are also conceivable:

- The composition of the injured worker population may have changed on observable dimensions, including demographics, wages, industry mix, or disability duration.
- The composition of the injured worker population may have changed on unobservable dimensions due to changes in claims-filing behavior over the business cycle.
- The effectiveness of medical care or rehabilitation may have changed.

Although we cannot conclusively test all of these potential explanations within the scope of this report, we can examine the importance of observable changes in composition. The hypotheses that the injured worker population shifted in unobservable ways or that the effectiveness of medical care or rehabilitation declined over this time period are more speculative, and we do not address them further in this report.

Rich information available in WCIS and the EDD base wage file allows us to examine whether concurrent changes in the composition of the PPD population might be confounded with aggregate trends, and whether the large changes observed in average outcomes appear to be driven by such compositional changes.

We begin our investigation by presenting summary statistics on a range of factors hypothesized to affect earnings, employment, and return to work following a workplace injury. These can be broadly classified into worker demographics, job and employer characteristics, firm dynamics, and injury characteristics. Table 4.2 presents the percentage female, the average age, and the age distribution for the overall injured worker population (column 1) and the three time periods defined above (columns 2–4). Compared with workers injured in 2005–2007,

---

[4]   As discussed in Chapter Three, the WCIS may be subject to underreporting among public-sector employees. Without an external source of data on the industrial composition of the full PPD population, it is not clear how to correct for this potential underreporting. A more worrisome problem would arise if the pattern of underreporting across industries varied over time, since this could create the appearance of overall trends even if none exist. In order to assess robustness to time-varying underreporting across industries, we recalculated the overall time profile of earnings loss by calculating industry-specific time profiles and then calculating a weighted average of these time profiles using statewide industry employment shares by quarter as weights. The resulting time profile of relative earnings looks very similar to results for the WCIS injury population, suggesting that our results are not driven by time-varying underreporting. See Appendix B for estimates.

Table 4.2
WCIS Injured Worker Demographics

	All Cases	Injury Year 2005–2007	Injury Year 2008–2009	Injury Year 2010–2012
Female (%)	41	40	42	43
Average Age	44.4	43.9	44.6	45.0
Age Distribution (%)				
16–20	1	1	1	1
21–25	5	5	5	5
26–30	8	8	8	8
31–35	9	10	9	9
36–40	12	13	12	11
41–45	15	16	15	13
46–50	16	17	17	16
51–55	16	15	16	16
56–60	11	10	12	12
61–65	5	5	5	6
66–70	1	1	2	2

NOTE: WCIS injured workers receiving PPD benefits 2005–2012.

workers injured in 2010–2012 are 1.1 years older on average (45.0 versus 43.9) and 3 percentage points more likely to be female. Research has shown that women experience larger post-injury earnings losses (Boden and Galizzi, 2003). There is evidence suggesting that older workers experience more severe injuries on average, although we are not aware of any studies on how the earnings loss resulting from an injury of a given severity varies with age (Silverstein, 2008).

Table 4.3 presents pre-injury annual earnings, post-injury control worker earnings, and the proportion of the sample falling into each quartile of the wage distribution. Inflation-adjusted annual earnings over the year prior to the injury for injured workers fell by about $1,500 (from $47,751 to $46,241) for the periods 2005–2007 and 2008–2009 and then fell by an additional $2,700 (to $43,050) for the 2008–2009 and 2010–2012 periods.[5] Remarkably, the decline in pre-injury wages among injured workers over recent years is not driven purely by wage growth failing to keep up with inflation. The average nominal pre-injury wage for injured workers actually declined between the recession period and the post-recession period, from $41,487 in 2008–2009 to $40,426 in the 2010–2012 periods. The distribution of workers by pre-injury wage quartile highlights that this change in the average is driven by a sizable increase for 2005–2007 and 2010–2012 (4.4 percentage points, or about 19 percent) in the fraction of workers with real pre-injury annual earnings in the lowest quartile.[6]

---

[5]   All dollar amounts have been inflated to constant 2014 dollars using the Urban Consumer Price Index so that income levels can be compared across years.

[6]   Income quartiles used in this report were defined by pooling all cases in the WCIS together (using weights to correct for match failure) and calculating quartiles of annual pre-injury earnings after inflating all earnings to real 2014 dollars. The income quartile cutoffs are defined using all workers with matched controls, whereas the sample used to analyze compositional changes is restricted to workers with complete data on all of the variables presented in Tables 4.2–4.4.

Table 4.3
WCIS Injured Worker Wages and Firm Characteristics

Sample Averages (Standard Deviations in Parentheses)	All Cases	Injury Year 2005–2007	Injury Year 2008–2009	Injury Year 2010–2012
Pre-injury wage*	$46,083 (36,137)	$47,751 (36,174)	$46,241 (36,449)	$43,556 (35,661)
Nominal pre-injury wage	$40,448 (31,769)	$39,823 (30,227)	$41,487 (32,654)	$40,426 (33,082)
Pre-injury job tenure (quarters)	5.92 (2.98)	5.74 (3.08)	5.96 (2.92)	6.12 (2.92)
Post-injury control wage*	$42,423 (36,167)	$45,013 (36,713)	$40,393 (36,131)	$40,505 (35,165)
Firm growth rate (%)	2.31 (16.57)	3.95 (16.20)	−0.90 (17.08)	2.79 (16.24)
Firm Separation Rate (%)	11.32 (9.59)	12.27 (9.97)	11.36 (9.40)	9.93 (9.01)
Percentage of Injured Workers				
First Quartile of Wages	24	23	23	27
Second Quartile of Wages	25	23	26	26
Third Quartile of Wages	25	26	25	24
Fourth Quartile of Wages	26	28	25	22
Pre-Injury Job Tenure (%)				
0–1 Quarters	14	16	12	13
2–3 Quarters	11	11	11	9
4–5 Quarters	9	9	9	8
6–7 Quarters	7	7	8	6
8 Quarters or More	60	58	60	64
Industry (%)				
Manufacturing	13	13	13	12
Transportation and Warehousing	5	5	6	5
Health Care	8	7	9	9
Public Administration	13	16	12	9
Education	6	6	6	7
Administrative and Support Services	3	3	3	3
Agriculture	13	12	13	13
Retail	5	4	5	6
Accommodation and Food Services	7	8	7	5
Construction	5	5	5	6
Wholesale	6	5	6	6
Other	16	14	17	18

Table 4.3—Continued

Sample Averages (Standard Deviations in Parentheses)	All Cases	Injury Year 2005–2007	Injury Year 2008–2009	Injury Year 2010–2012
Firm Size (%)				
Firm Size: 1–10 Employees	3	2	3	3
Firm Size: 11–50 Employees	15	13	15	17
Firm Size: 51–100 Employees	9	10	9	7
Firm Size: 101–500 Employees	17	17	18	18
Firm Size: 501–1000 Employees	8	8	8	8
Firm Size: 1,001–5,000 Employees	20	19	20	21
Firm Size: Over 5,000 Employees	28	32	27	25
Firm Growth Rate (%)				
−30% or Lower	3	2	4	2
−30% to −10%	12	9	19	10
−10% to −0.5%	28	23	31	34
−0.5% to 0.5%	7	6	7	8
0.5% to 10%	31	39	25	26
10% to 30%	12	13	9	13
30% or Higher	7	7	5	7
Firm Separation Rate (%)				
4.4% or Less	24	23	22	27
4.4% to 8%	25	22	24	29
8% to 14%	26	25	28	25
14% or Higher	26	31	26	19

NOTES: * Annual earnings reported in inflation-adjusted real 2014 dollars unless otherwise noted.

The injured worker's tenure at the at-injury firm is likely to be an important predictor of earnings losses and return to work. The effect of tenure on earnings loss is not clear a priori. Workers with higher job tenure may have a stronger relationship with their employers and may therefore be more likely to return to work and receive needed accommodation or workplace modification. By the same token, workers with higher job tenure may have more specialized skills and thus may have more to lose if their employment relationship is disrupted by injury. We measure pre-injury job tenure by counting the number of consecutive quarters of employment at the at-injury firm preceding the quarter of injury. In order to define job tenure consistently across all cohorts in our sample, the highest category of pre-injury job tenure is eight quarters (two years) of pre-injury employment. Table 4.3 shows that the majority of injured workers (60 percent across all years) have job tenure of two years or higher at the time of injury. Workers injured during and after the recession have higher pre-injury job tenure: the fraction with two years or more of tenure at the at-injury firm increases from 58 percent in 2005–2007 to 60 percent in 2008–2009 and then to 64 percent in 2010–2012. Increases in job tenure among workers injured during the recession might be expected as a consequence of compositional changes in the broader labor force. Some research on the relationship between injury rates and the business cycle finds that weak labor market conditions deter the filing of workers' compensation claims, and it is plausible that this effect might be more pronounced among workers with lower job tenure (Boone and van Ours, 2006). On this view, the sharper increase in job tenure among permanently disabled workers during the recovery period is more surprising and may be a symptom of the weak labor market recovery.

Table 4.3 also reports data on employer characteristics known or hypothesized to affect earnings and employment outcomes. Known factors include industrial composition and firm size distribution, while less-studied but potentially important factors include two measures of employment dynamics: the firm-level growth rate and the firm-level separation rate.

Several notable compositional changes are apparent. The shares of public administration, construction, and manufacturing workers decline, while the shares of industries including health care, education, and accommodations and food services increase. At-injury employers also appear to be slightly smaller on average after the recession, with the proportion of injured workers coming from the largest firms (5,000 or more employees) falling from 32 percent before the recession to 25 percent after the recession. Firm size is a well-established determinant of safety: Mendeloff et al. (2006) confirmed earlier evidence that smaller establishments had higher fatality rates than larger establishments, controlling for industry. They established that it was the size of the establishment, not the size of the firm, which had, by far, the greatest role.[7] (While we measure the size of the firm, firm size and establishment size are correlated.) However, the influence of firm size on outcomes after an injury has occurred has been studied less widely. A key reason may be that workers' compensation information rarely has a good link to employer size. Some studies have found higher total disability durations at smaller firms, but some studies have failed to support this finding (Hunt and Habeck, 1993; Cheadle et al., 1994; Galizzi and Boden, 1996).[8] An earlier RAND study showed that smaller firms were less likely to have formal return to work programs (Seabury et al., 2011).

Table 4.3 also provides evidence of other changes in the mix of at-injury employers over the period 2005–2012. The growth rate of employment over the year preceding an injury fell from 4.0 percent per year in 2005–2007 to slightly negative (–0.9 percent) in 2008–2009 before rebounding to 2.8 percent in 2010–2012. The average turnover rate for at-injury firms, meanwhile, fell from 12.3 percent to 9.9 percent from 2005–2007 to 2010–2012. We hypothesize several channels through which firm-level employment dynamics could be important determinants of earnings losses. Since earnings losses are defined relative to the earnings of uninjured controls at the same employer, factors such as employer growth and the turnover rate that may affect earnings growth for uninjured workers will mechanically affect wage losses.[9] Controlling for industry will capture much of this variation, but measures of firm dynamics may reflect differences in the human resources strategies and importance of firm-specific human capital across different employers within the same industry. Since relative post-injury return to the at-injury employer continues to decline over time for injured workers, it is likely that the disruption of the employer-employee relationship contributes to long-term earnings losses. The employment growth rate and the turnover rate may both contain information about the potential earnings growth lost due to an injury that is not captured by other control vari-

---

[7]   A "firm" refers to a business that may comprise multiple locations, or "establishments."

[8]   Cheadle et al. (1994) found higher TTD durations for firms with fewer than 50 employees. However, Hunt and Habeck (1993) and Galizzi and Boden (1996) found little or no effect.

[9]   See Anderson et al. (1994) for an overview of economic theories of the job turnover rate.

Table 4.4
WCIS Injured Worker Severity

Characteristic	All Cases	Injury Year 2005–2007	Injury Year 2008–2009	Injury Year 2010–2012
Weeks of Total Temporary Disability	27.4	26.5	29.6	26.9
Number of Permanent Impairments	0.9	0.8	1.0	1.1

NOTES: The average TTD duration reported in this table was winsorized at the maximum TTD duration of 104 weeks, a process that affected slightly under 5,000 cases. WCIS impairment rating data may be reserving estimates that are not revised and therefore do not necessarily reflect the eventual disability status of injured workers.

ables. Finally, the turnover rate may also be informative about the importance of job-specific expertise and training at the firm in question. The importance of such expertise, which economists refer to as "firm-specific human capital," should affect an employer's incentives to rehabilitate and retain an injured worker. While, as discussed above, the injured worker's job tenure captures the potential for the individual worker to have accumulated firm-specific human capital, the turnover rate is likely to contain additional information about how firm-specific human capital is valued by the employer and thus may predict differences in earnings losses among workers with the same job tenure at different employers.

Finally, the severity of the average PPD worker's impairment may also change over the business cycle. Numerous studies have documented that the incidence rate of workers' compensation claims is related to the business cycle (Boone and van Ours, 2006; Asfaw, Pana-Cryan, and Rosa, 2011; Boone et al., 2011).[10] These studies tend to find that business cycle effects are less pronounced or nonexistent for fatal and severe injuries. The implications of these findings for the overall PPD population are unclear, however, since not all PPD cases originate with severe or traumatic injuries. Therefore, we cannot rule out a priori the possibility that the composition of permanent impairments shifted toward types of health conditions with more severe consequences, or that the average severity of cases changed during the recession.

It is difficult to measure the severity of impairment directly, but several useful proxy variables are available in the WCIS. One useful measure that is reliably observed is whether claimants receive temporary total disability payments, and what duration of total disability is implied by those payments. We also control for the body part identified as the site of the initial injury. While it might be preferable to control for the type of permanent impairment, detailed information about the type of permanent impairment is not reported in the WCIS for approximately one-third of workers who receive PPD benefit payments. Both measures are summarized in Table 4.4. Both measures suggest greater severity during the Great Recession, but implied disability durations decline slightly in 2010–2012 while the number of reported impairments remains elevated.[11]

---

[10] See Asfaw, Pana-Cryan, and Rosa (2011) for evidence describing the association between non-fatal injury rates and the business cycle in the United States. Boone and van Ours (2006) and Boone et al. (2011) find similar patterns using data from Europe.

[11] We emphasize that these are at best very noisy measures of disability severity due to limitations of the WCIS data. Additional details on disability duration, including the distribution of body parts of injury, are presented in Appendix B.

Table 4.5
Which Factors Predict Earnings Losses?

Explanatory Variables	Percentage of Explained Variation	
	Second-Year Earnings Loss	Third-Year Earnings Loss
Temporary disability duration	54.3	45.5
Body part of injury (FROI)	9.8	10.1
Pre-injury wage	4.2	5.3
Age	4.0	12.9
Industry	3.0	4.3
Pre-injury job tenure	2.4	2.3
Firm separation rate	1.7	2.9
Firm size	0.8	0.6
Firm growth rate	0.6	1.1
Quarter of injury	0.4	0.4
Number of permanent impairments	0.1	0.2
Gender	0.0	0.1
R-Squared	12.3	9.2

NOTES: Table reports partial sum of squares as percentage of model sum of squares from ANOVA for individual-level proportional earnings losses measured in the second and third post-injury years. See Appendix B for details on the construction of individual-level earnings loss measures. All predictors are statistically significant at the 0.1-percent level.

by case characteristics, the majority is driven by differences in injury severity, economic status, age, and job characteristics. Even though the Great Recession was associated with dramatic shifts in average wage loss, differences between workers injured at a point in time are dramatically larger than differences over time in outcomes for similarly situated workers.

The analysis in Table 4.5 is informative about the fraction of total variation in outcomes due to different factors: it tells us that a very small share of the total variation observed among all PPD cases from 2005 to 2012 is predicted by the injury date when other factors are also accounted for. However, these results do not tell us what fraction of the change in *average* outcomes between the pre-recession and post-recession periods is explained by the date of injury after controlling for these other factors. The relatively small proportion of variation explained by the date of injury tells us, instead, that there is a large amount of dispersion in earnings losses among injuries occurring at the same time, and that other case-mix adjusters (such as TTD duration and earnings loss) are capable of explaining much of this dispersion.

A different method is needed to analyze changes in the average outcome between injuries before versus after the recession. We build on the regression specifications used for case-mix adjustment to decompose the change in average earnings loss into a portion that is predicted by compositional changes and a remainder that is attributed to time effects. Table 4.6 presents the results of analyses conducted for three outcomes measured in the second post-injury year: average earnings losses, median earnings losses, and the reduction in employment at the end of

Table 4.6
Contribution of Compositional Changes to Change in Average Outcomes During and After the Great Recession

Fraction of Average Change Explained by . . .	Average % Earnings Loss	Median % Earnings Loss	Reduction in Employment
Recession	53	63	57
Compositional effects	47	37	43

NOTES: Median % earnings loss decomposition calculated using DeNardo-Fortin-Lemieux reweighting method. Reduction in employment calculated using Oaxaca-Blinder decomposition for difference between individual employment and control worker average employment. See Appendix B for details.

the second post-injury year. The methods in the table are based on a binary division of injury dates into injuries occurring during and after the Great Recession (2008–2012) and injuries occurring before the Great Recession (2005–2007).[19]

The results in Table 4.6 quantify the contribution of compositional changes to the time profile of earnings losses observed between 2005 and 2012. Compositional changes account for 46 percent of the decrease in relative earnings that followed the Great Recession.

A drawback of using relative earnings calculated at the individual level as an outcome variable is that outliers caused by very small values of control worker earnings can lead to noisy results. Table 4.6 therefore reports two alternative decompositions that should not be affected by outliers in individual-level relative earnings and related technical problems. Compositional changes account for somewhat less (35 percent) of the change in median relative earnings over this period, and an intermediate portion (40 percent) of the change in the post-injury reduction in employment. Similar calculations that focus only on data from the post-recession (2010–2012) period and the pre-recession period yield estimates of the compositional effect that are slightly (1 to 4 percentage points) smaller but otherwise very similar.[20]

Taken together, the results in Table 4.6 indicate that between 37 percent and 47 percent of the deterioration in outcomes for injured workers that followed the Great Recession was due to compositional changes.[21] We view this as a meaningful fraction of the overall change in average outcomes, but we also view this as indicating that the effect of the recession on outcomes independently of compositional changes was quite substantial.

Because our data report earnings on a quarterly basis, it is not clear whether the downward trend in pre-injury earnings is driven by a shift toward lower-wage workers or by reductions in hours worked. The number of workers who report working part-time for economic reasons such as slack business conditions doubled from 2005 to 2009 and has receded more slowly than the overall unemployment rate, so it is plausible that reduced hours among workers

---

[19] See Appendix B for details and for estimates that compare only post-recession (2010–2012) injuries to pre-recession (2005–2007) injuries.

[20] See Appendix B for details.

[21] For the average change in earnings and employment, it is possible to decompose the compositional effect into contributions associated with specific groups of variables. The compositional changes that were most important in predicting the decline in relative earnings in 2008 and later were (in descending order of importance) increases in injury severity, lower pre-injury wages, declines in the job separation rate, and increases in the age at injury. Injury severity comprises TTD duration, number of permanent impairments, and the body part of injury. See Appendix Table B.10 for detailed estimates.

contributed to lower pre-injury earnings (Bureau of Labor Statistics, 2015). However, analysis of data reporting hours worked together with work injury occurrence would be necessary to determine if this is actually the case. Some important questions raised by these findings are whether these workers are likely to have weaker ties to their employers, or if employers have weaker incentives to rehabilitate and invest in return to work in a slack labor market.

An alternative explanation for the compositional shift toward lower-wage workers emanates from the workers' compensation system itself. The real value of PPD benefits for higher-wage workers has been falling over time because the weekly maximum wage was not indexed to inflation prior to passage of S.B. 863. For workers above the weekly maximum wage, the cumulative effect of inflation between 2005 and 2013 was equivalent to a 15.5-percent cut in benefits. The incentive for higher-wage workers to pursue PPD benefits therefore weakened over time. While there is a sizable research literature demonstrating that TTD claiming is responsive to benefit generosity, the evidence on PPD is less conclusive.

Because we took earnings, job tenure, and employer into account in selecting matched control workers, the findings discussed so far on the relationship between wages and employer characteristics on earnings losses can be interpreted as capturing the causal effects of job and firm characteristics on earnings losses. Our model also included controls for a range of additional variables related to demographics and injury characteristics that were not explicitly used in the matching process. Estimated coefficients on these variables should be interpreted with more caution, but these variables can nonetheless be used as case-mix adjusters to evaluate the impact of compositional changes in the pattern of earnings losses over the period of our study. In interpreting these estimates, it is also important to understand that the estimates presented in Figures 4.5–4.6 represent the relationship between pre-injury earnings and proportional post-injury earnings *holding all other factors constant*, meaning that this pattern is not driven by differences in injury severity, industry, job tenure, or in any of the other variables included in our analysis.

CHAPTER FIVE

Wage Replacement and Benefit Adequacy Under S.B. 899 and S.B. 863

Chapter Four documented recent declines in the earnings and employment of permanently disabled workers. In this chapter, we compare earnings losses to benefits and analyze the negative impact of the Great Recession on the degree to which PPD benefits protect workers against interruptions in income caused by their injuries. We also simulate the changes enacted under S.B. 863 and evaluate the effects of these reforms on wage replacement. In addition to analyzing benefit adequacy, we document the spread of alternative rating procedures allowed under a series of WCAB rulings beginning in 2009 and estimate the potential influence of these alternative rating procedures on benefits. Specifically, we address the following questions:

- How did ratings and benefits under S.B. 899 evolve between 2005 and 2012?
- What fraction of earnings losses were replaced by PPD benefits for workers injured between 2005 and 2012?
- What would wage replacement rates have been over the period 2005–2012 if S.B. 863 had been in place?
- Which changes in ratings and benefits under S.B. 863 are likely to have the most important effect on wage replacement rates?
- What is the potential effect of alternative rating procedures on ratings and benefits?

To address these questions, we measure trends in PD ratings and statutory benefits among cases rated at the DEU under S.B. 899, and we combine these data with our earnings loss data to report wage replacement rates for the overall PPD population.

Ratings Data from the Disability Evaluation Unit

We use data from the state DEU instead of the WCIS as our primary data source on ratings and statutory benefits. While we consider the WCIS the most representative and timely data source for identifying workers who receive PPD benefits in California's workers' compensation system, our ability to analyze PPD benefits and ratings in the WCIS is severely limited by several aspects of the data. As discussed in Chapter Four, about one-third of injuries for the years 2005–2012 that are reported as receiving PPD benefits in the WCIS do not have any data on impairment ratings. While impairment ratings are more frequently reported alongside benefits in recent years, the changing fraction of cases with impairment ratings reported undermines our confidence in trends calculated using the WCIS. The DEU data also has limitations, but it is the most authoritative source for detailed and accurate data on disability ratings.

Before turning to the analysis of trends in ratings and benefits, it is necessary to discuss some institutional details of the DEU that are important for understanding our data on ratings and benefits. Many, if not most, workers' compensation cases with PPD are never rated by the DEU. DEU ratings are performed at the request of one of the parties to the case or, under some circumstances, a workers' compensation judge. There is considerable variation in the time it takes for a DEU rating to be requested, and cases accordingly may not reach the DEU for some time after injury. The lag between injury and rating requires that analysts take considerable care in using DEU data to measure trends, as we discuss below.

Table 5.1 presents summary statistics on cases rated at the DEU. The first column (labeled "All Available Ratings") reports averages for ratings performed at the DEU by May 2015 of cases with injury dates between 2005 and 2012 and complete data on final ratings and rating type. The remaining columns of the table (labeled "Constant-Maturity Sample") report averages for the sample of ratings that we use to measure trends by injury date over the 2005–2012 period. The second column reports overall averages for this sample of ratings, while the third through fifth columns report averages disaggregated by the type of rating.

When measuring trends in the DEU, it is important to work with a *constant-maturity* sample of cases, meaning a sample of cases that reaches the DEU within a fixed length of time after the injury date. Because cases can take so long to reach the DEU, it is not possible to

Table 5.1
Summary Statistics for Sample of DEU Ratings Used to Measure Trends

Characteristic	All Ratings	Constant-Maturity Sample (rated within 851 days of injury)		
		All Ratings	Consult Ratings	Summary Ratings	Formal Ratings
Number of Ratings	191,477	118,524	55,461	62,193	870
Percentage of Constant-Maturity Ratings			47%	52%	1%
Percentage of All Available Ratings			55%	44%	1%
Final Rating Before Apportionment*	20.3	16.5	21.4	12.0	29.0
Final Rating After Apportionment	19.6	16.0	20.9	11.4	26.8
Statutory Benefit at Maximum Weekly Wage					
Without Life Pension	$21,432	$15,953	$22,433	$9,932	$33,336
Including Life Pension**	$23,098	$16,654	$23,698	$10,080	$37,611
Average Number of Rated Impairments	1.6	1.5	1.7	1.2	1.9
Days to First Rating					
Average	817	528	567	492	598
Median	696	531	578	486	632

* Row excludes 538 cases without apportionment information reported.

** Includes discounted present value of life pension (see Chapter Six for details).

NOTES: DEU records excluded if data on final rating after apportionment, body system of impairment, or rating type is missing or invalid. Column labeled "All Maturities" presents summary statistics for injuries occurring between 2005 and 2012 that were rated at the DEU before May 2015. Columns labeled "Constant-Maturity Sample" present cases rated within 851 days of injury, allowing comparable measurement of ratings and benefit trends by date of injury through the end of 2012.

observe an entire cohort of injured workers until many years have passed since the time of injury. For example, 43 percent of cases with injury dates between 2005 and 2009 took 900 days or longer to reach the DEU; a substantial fraction of cases take five years or longer. For more recent injury years, then, the fraction of cases that can be observed in the DEU data steadily declines in a nonrandom way unless we restrict attention to a constant-maturity sample.

The first two columns of Table 5.1 illustrate the tradeoff involved in using a constant-maturity sample. Restricting attention to a constant-maturity sample that allows measurement of trends through the end of 2012 excludes over one-third of the ratings performed at the DEU on injuries between 2005 and 2012. The remaining cases have substantially lower impairment ratings and benefits, reflecting the fact that more severe cases take longer to reach the DEU.

The characteristics of cases differ in important ways across the three types of ratings performed at the DEU. These types are Consult ratings (47 percent of ratings examined in Table 5.1), Summary ratings (52 percent), and Formal ratings (1 percent). Workers evaluated by Consult ratings have legal representation, whereas workers with Summary ratings are unrepresented. Formal ratings, which are far less common, are performed at the request of a workers' compensation administrative law judge to help resolve issues in a disputed claim before the WCAB and may or may not be represented. Table 5.1 presents summary statistics separately for these three types of ratings. Consult ratings yield substantially higher impairment ratings than do Summary ratings. Table 5.1 shows that the average final rating before apportionment is 21.4 for Consult ratings, over 75 percent higher than the average final rating of 12 for Summary ratings. Consult ratings have more rated impairments on average (1.7 impairments for Consult ratings versus 1.2 for Summary ratings). Formal ratings represent a small fraction of all ratings examined in Table 5.1 (1.0 percent), although they appear to be differentially severe and complex cases, with higher final ratings.

Table 5.1 also presents average statutory benefit amounts based on final ratings. These amounts represent the undiscounted total value of PPD payments mandated by the Labor Code, and are our primary measure of benefit generosity. Because the DEU does not have reliable reporting of weekly pre-injury wages, the benefit amounts presented here are calculated at the statutory maximum. The average benefit, in constant 2014 dollars, was $16,654 for the sample of DEU cases we use to estimate trends. Average benefits differ between Summary, Consult, and Formal ratings in line with the differences in impairment ratings.

The last rows of Table 5.1 report the mean and median number of days between the date of injury and the date of the first rating at the DEU for the constant-maturity subsample of cases we use to estimate trends in replacement rates for the DEU. This subsample of cases is restricted to injuries that are rated at the DEU within 851 days of the injury date so that we can directly measure trends through the end of 2012. Among this subsample of cases, the average time before a case in our sample is rated is about 18 months (528 days). In contrast, the average time between the date of injury and the first rating at the DEU for all available injuries occurring from 2005 to 2012 is over two years (817 days).

If the duration between an injury and a case's first rating at the DEU were random, restriction to a constant-maturity sample of cases would not limit our ability to measure trends in outcomes. Unfortunately, this is not the case: more severe and complex injuries systematically take longer after the date of injury to reach the DEU.[1] Outcomes for severe injuries in

---

[1] Final impairment ratings increase by 0.72 percentage points on average with each 100 days of time between the injury and the rating. See Appendix C for details.

the years immediately preceding enactment of S.B. 863 cannot currently be studied using the DEU data because many of these cases have not yet received any ratings and thus are not observed. The average levels of ratings and benefits described in this chapter accordingly may underestimate the averages observed among the full PPD population because the most severe cases are systematically excluded. Even so, trends among less severe cases are informative about how the disability rating process—meaning the collective behavior of workers, employers, insurers, doctors, lawyers, and judges—evolved over the eight years between S.B. 899 and S.B. 863.[2] In spite of the limitation of our measured trends, we believe they may reflect the dynamics that will play out when the most severe cases from the later years of the S.B. 899 era eventually reach the DEU.

Trends in Ratings and Benefits Under S.B. 899

The sharp reductions in earnings documented in Chapter Four would imply reductions in benefit adequacy if benefits remained constant over the 2005–2012 time period. Even though there were no statutory changes to benefits between 2005 and 2012, several other factors may have led to changes in the level of benefits over this time period.

First, we find that average disability ratings increased substantially between 2005 and 2012. This is consistent with some of the compositional changes documented in Chapter Four, where we noted that WCIS data on TTD duration and number of impairments suggest that injuries may have been slightly more severe during and after the Great Recession. Also, workers injured during and after the recession were older on average than those injured before the recession. Injury severity and age should both directly lead to higher impairment ratings, and so we would expect to see some of the decline in earnings offset by increased benefits.

In addition to changes in the claimant population, the behavior of parties to the disability rating process can evolve over time such that ratings tend to creep upward. Physicians and applicants' attorneys may have taken some time after adoption of the AMA *Guides* in 2005 to learn how best to apply the new rating system. We might expect ratings to trend upward over time as knowledge about the rating system diffuses among doctors and attorneys, even if factors explicitly accounted for in the rating process are held constant.

Figure 5.1 presents average trends in final ratings on injuries occurring for the period 2005–2012 that were rated at the DEU within 851 days of injury, stratified by rating type. Besides having higher ratings on average, cases with legal representation also display a large upward trend beginning around the start of 2007. Between 2005 and 2012, the average final rating on a Consult rating evaluated at constant maturity increased from 18.9 to 22.9 for a cumulative percentage increase of 21 percent. Final ratings rose less sharply among Summary ratings between 2005 and 2012, from 10.9 to 12.4 for a cumulative percentage increase of 12 percent.

Another factor, however, may tend to reduce benefits relative to losses over time, offsetting the effect of higher ratings. This is the influence of wage growth and inflation on the real value of the maximum weekly wage allowable in calculating PPD benefits. PPD benefits are capped by a provision specifying a maximum dollar value for the weekly wage used to calculate

---

[2]   In Appendix C, we compare trends in wage loss and benefits among low- and high-maturity cases for an earlier period of time when higher-maturity cases can also be consistently observed. Trends in both wage loss and benefits moved in the same direction for low- and high-maturity cases with injury dates from 2005 to 2009.

Table 5.2
Almaraz Cases as Percentage of Each Rating Type by Transaction Date

Calendar Year of Rating	Rating Type		
	Summary	Consult	Formal
2005	0	0	0
2006	0	0	0
2007	0	0	0
2008	0	0	0
2009	1.3	6.9	0.9
2010	3.0	17.5	5.2
2011	6.8	23.0	6.8
2012	18.0	25.0	5.2
2013	19.5	25.6	7.9
2014	20.0	25.8	9.9
2015 (thru 5/13/15)	19.1	27.1	2.3

NOTE: Rating type determined by DEU coding for latest rating, chronologically. *Almaraz* rating determined by identification of specific phrases used by DEU raters in the final rating text. If any rating included the identifying text, the claim was identified as *Almaraz.*

We have not incorporated *Almaraz* ratings into our main analysis of statutory benefits and wage replacement rates in this chapter because the DEU data do not provide information about whether *Almaraz* ratings were based on underlying reports that met the legal requirements placed on evaluating physicians' opinions as outlined in *Almaraz/Guzman.* Instead, we conduct an analysis at the end of this chapter that illustrates the potential effect of alternative ratings on indemnity benefits.

There was a second important case law decision affecting application of the AMA *Guides* during the period between S.B. 899 and S.B. 863. The WCAB's ruling in *Ogilvie vs. City and County of San Francisco* introduced a different type of alternative rating that essentially stepped completely outside the AMA *Guides.* These ratings are not thought to be frequent, in part because they require extensive expert testimony. And these ratings are almost never visible in the DEU data. In addition, the influence of the *Ogilvie* decision was eliminated by statutory changes under S.B. 863. Consequently, the effect of the *Ogilvie* decision was not evaluated. This will tend to bias the estimated indemnity down by an unknown but probably limited amount.

To sum up, ratings performed at the DEU indicate that there was a steady upward trend in ratings and statutory benefits for permanently disabled workers injured between 2005 and 2012. Statutory benefits for low-maturity cases that can be compared across time over this entire period may have increased by 19 percent to 28 percent between the 2005 and 2012 injury years: higher ratings clearly outweighed the effects of inflation, especially for represented cases, which constitute a majority of PPD cases in California. These increases in ratings and benefits have the potential to offset the increased earnings losses observed in Chapter Four, at least in part. In the remainder of this chapter, we compare benefits for permanently disabled workers to earnings losses in order to assess trends in benefit adequacy under S.B. 899 and the effect of S.B. 863.

Definition and Measurement of Benefit Adequacy

A goal of workers' compensation policy is to protect workers against income losses caused by accidents. The extent to which benefits successfully indemnify workers against losses is known as the *adequacy* of benefits. Benefit adequacy has been widely accepted as a normative benchmark for evaluating workers' compensation policy since at least the National Commission Report of 1972 (National Commission, 1972; Peterson et al., 1998; Boden and Galizzi, 1999; Reville, Boden, et al., 2001; Reville et al., 2005; Seabury et al., 2011). The National Commission did not make specific recommendations for permanent partial disability benefits that would permit a translation of providing "substantial protection against interruption of income" into a numerical or quantitative standard. However, for temporary total and permanent total disability, the commission recommended that, subject to the state's maximum weekly benefits, the disability benefits be at least two-thirds of the worker's pre-injury *gross weekly wage* or four-fifths (80 percent) of the worker's *after-tax* income.

If a similar degree of protection were provided for permanent partial disability as for permanent total disability, then after the date of MMI, the PPD benefits should replace two-thirds of the difference between the worker's expected gross earnings (the earnings that a worker would have earned had they not been injured) and the worker's actual gross earnings. Alternatively stated, benefits are adequate if the replacement rate—the PPD benefits divided by the earnings losses experienced by injured workers—is at least 66 2/3 percent. The replacement rate of 66 2/3 percent (or two-thirds) of lost wages (measured before payroll deductions for taxes or other items) as the measure of adequacy represents the majority position of a National Academy of Social Insurance report on the adequacy of permanent partial disability benefits (Hunt, 2004).

As in much previous research, we focus on the *wage replacement rate*, or the fraction of earnings losses due to injury that is compensated by PPD benefits, as our measure of benefit adequacy. Because workers' compensation benefits are not subject to income and payroll taxes, we report after-tax replacement rates throughout this report.[7] Applying income and payroll taxes has a sizable influence on post-injury wages: average control worker earnings in the first post-injury year are 31.2 percent lower after taxes than before taxes. It is worth noting that the percentage reduction in average income due to taxes is higher than the tax rate faced by the typical worker. If we calculate the average tax rate for each worker in our sample, we find that the median worker in the sample had an average tax rate of 25.9 percent (17.3 percent excluding payroll taxes).

---

[7]   Our income tax calculator includes federal and California income taxes. We approximate income tax liability assuming that workers have no non-income labor sources and that all workers file singly and take the standard deduction. These assumptions are necessary because we lack data on non-labor income, family structure, and homeownership and other deductible expenditures. Because our follow-up periods for workers are based on the quarter of injury and do not align with tax years for the majority of our sample, we tax income received over a period that spans two tax years under the rates in place at the end of the period.

    Payroll taxes include both Social Security and Medicare contributions (7.65 percent) and state disability insurance (SDI) contributions (between 0.8 percent and 1.2 percent). Yearly changes in the taxable income limit for payroll taxes were accounted for, as were fluctuations in the SDI contribution rate.

We calculate wage replacement rates as the ratio of statutory benefits to estimated earnings losses over the first five years following the date of injury. Because we do not have five years of follow-up data for recent cohorts, we use a sample of injuries from 2008 and earlier to estimate the ratio between five-year earnings losses and earnings losses in the second year.[8] It is important to note that these wage replacement rates are a benchmark intended to facilitate comparison across alternative policies and trends over time, and are likely to understate lifetime earnings losses for many workers because earnings losses may persist well beyond five years. This is particularly true for the most severe injuries.

Anticipated Effects of S.B. 863 on Benefit Adequacy

S.B. 863 implemented several changes to the PD rating system and also changed the relationship between impairment ratings and indemnity benefits. The ratings changes included elimination of certain secondary "add-on" impairments, elimination of the 15-percent bump-up/bump-down incentives for post-injury employment, and increases in the FEC adjustment factors. We defer detailed discussion of these provisions until we examine ratings in Chapter Six. In this chapter, we focus on the net effect of these provisions on final ratings and benefits, which was expected to be a sizable increase in indemnity payments.

In addition to changing the ratings process, S.B. 863 included increases in the level of indemnity benefits available to the majority of workers. The minimum weekly benefit was increased from $130 to $160. For workers with ratings less than 70 percent, the maximum benefit was increased in two steps from $230 per week to $290 per week. And for workers with ratings between 70 percent and 99 percent the maximum was increased from $270 per week to $290 per week. Because over two-thirds (68.7 percent) of injured workers had weekly wages greater than $405 per week, raising the maximum benefit rate is likely to have a substantial effect. Only 6 percent of workers are affected by the increase in the minimum benefit.

In addition to these changes in impairment ratings and benefits, S.B. 863 added a new benefit called the Return-to-Work Benefit for selected workers with permanent partial disabilities. As implemented by the DWC, this benefit is paid to workers who applied for and received a Supplemental Job Displacement Benefit voucher. Permanently impaired workers are eligible for the SJDB voucher if their employers are unable to offer them jobs that meet their work restrictions and that pay near their pre-injury wages. As currently implemented, the benefit pays $5,000 to each eligible worker that applies.

We simulate the influence that these provisions of S.B. 863 would have had on benefits had they been in place over the period 2005–2012. Specifically, we address the following questions:

- What would wage replacement rates have been over the period 2005–2012 if S.B. 863 had been in place?
- Which changes in ratings and benefits under S.B. 863 are likely to have the most important effect on wage replacement rates?

---

[8] This factor is 4.74. Proportional earnings losses are flat after the second year, but the dollar value of earnings losses diminishes over time as control worker earnings revert toward a long-run average as discussed in Chapter 3. See Appendix D for further details.

To address these questions, we analyze three provisions (changes to the minimum and maximum benefits, changes to the FEC, and elimination of specific add-on impairments) of S.B. 863 separately by simulating two levels of statutory benefits for each case in the DEU. First, to capture the effect of the benefit increase, we calculate benefits under the S.B. 863 weekly maximum using ratings actually calculated under S.B. 899. Then, to capture the full effect of the rating and benefit changes, we use detailed information on impairment ratings to recalculate final ratings under S.B. 863 and recalculate benefits under the S.B. 863 maximum benefit. Finally, we examine earnings at the at-injury employer following the date of maximum medical improvement as reported in the WCIS to approximate eligibility for the return to work benefit. This procedure is likely to overstate eligibility for the benefit because some separations from the at-injury employer may be voluntary, and so we view our estimates as providing an upper bound for the effect of the return to work benefit on adequacy.

S.B. 863 involved two other potentially important changes to the impairment rating system that are more difficult to analyze. First, the bill eliminated language that was key to the *Ogilvie* decision, theoretically making it impossible to challenge the AMA *Guides* ratings through claims of higher wage loss.[9] These ratings, while likely quite high, were thought to be very infrequent. They are also not visible in the DEU or WCIS data.

Second, as discussed above, S.B. 863 added LC4660.1(h) explicitly acknowledging in statute the application of the *Almaraz/Guzman* series of decisions.[10] It is unknown if this will affect the frequency of alternative ratings, which are typically substantially higher than ratings under the AMA *Guides*. We revisit the question of how alternative ratings could affect benefits at the end of this chapter.

Benefit Adequacy Under S.B. 899 and S.B. 863

Table 5.3 reports estimated five-year earnings losses and benefits for the WCIS sample for 2005–2012. As shown in Chapter Four, after-tax earnings losses increased sharply in the Great Recession and remained elevated during the early years of the economic recovery. We estimate that earnings losses over the first five post-injury years would be $40,778 for the average worker injured over the period 2005–2012, increasing from $36,238 before the recession to $45,484 after the recession. We estimate that statutory benefits for the WCIS PPD population increased less sharply than suggested by the trends in the DEU reported above, growing from $23,285 for injuries in 2005–2007 to $24,357 for injuries in 2008–2009, and then declining slightly in 2010–2012, to $23,793.

Table 5.3 also includes figures on the total amount of PPD indemnity benefits and PPD settlements paid to date as of extraction of WCIS data in September 2014. Averaged over the entire 2005–2012 time period, paid benefits are just 52 percent of statutory benefits. This low

---

[9] LC 4660 (a) was changed, removing the reference to future earning capacity that triggered *Ogilvie*. 4660(a) was changed to LC 4660.1(a) ("In determining the percentages of permanent disability, account shall be taken of the nature of the physical injury or disfigurement, the occupation of the injured employee, and his or her age at the time of the injury, consideration being given to an employee's diminished future earning capacity").

[10] SEC. 60. Section 4660.1 is added to the Labor Code, to read, "4660.1. This section shall apply to injuries occurring on or after January 1, 2013. . . . 4660.1. (h) In enacting the act adding this section, it is not the intent of the Legislature to overrule the holding in Milpitas Unified School District v. Workers' Comp. Appeals Bd. (Guzman) (2010) 187 Cal.App.4th 808."

lated using S.B. 899 ratings with the S.B. 863 maximum wage. The black line, meanwhile, shows the full effect of the ratings changes and benefit increases enacted under S.B. 863. While all three lines (mechanically) reflect the effect of the earnings loss trends reported in Chapter Four, both the increased maximum wage and the changes to ratings translate into sizable increases in wage replacement rates.

Our estimate of the statutory after-tax wage replacement rate for all workers injured for the years 2005–2012 is 58.8 percent. For these workers, the S.B. 863 weekly maximum would have increased after-tax wage replacement rates to 69.2 percent, while the combined effect of rating changes and the weekly maximum would have increased benefits to 76.8 percent of lost wages over the first five post-injury years. The higher weekly maximum wage would have increased benefits by about 10.4 percentage points, while the changes to the rating system (combined with the benefit increase) would have led to a further increase of 7.5 percentage points. The return to work benefit, depicted in the black line on Figure 5.5, increases the after-tax wage replacement rate by an additional 3.5 percentage points.

The combined effect of the three S.B. 863 provisions modeled here will be a substantial increase in after-tax wage replacement rates for permanently disabled workers. Had all three provisions been in place over 2005–2012, wage replacement rates would have been 24.7 percentage points (39 percent) higher for workers injured in 2005–2007, 20.5 percentage points (36 percent) higher for workers injured in 2008–2009, and 17.4 percentage points (33 percent) higher for workers injured in 2010–2012. The declining influence of S.B. 863 on wage replacement rates is in part a mechanical consequence of greater earnings losses in recent years (which increase the denominator of the wage replacement rate). It may also reflect the reduced influence of the hike in the maximum weekly wage, which is driven by the lower portion of workers constrained by the weekly maximum. In contrast to the weekly maximum and the changes to ratings, which have smaller effects (in percentage points) on the wage replacement rate after the recession, the effect of the return to work fund remains nearly constant in magnitude over the 2005–2012 period.

To assess the robustness of our conclusions, we present several alternative estimates of trends in benefit adequacy in Appendix C, including estimates that focus only on a constant-maturity subset of cases from the DEU. We also report estimates for the WCIS that use different assumptions in estimating statutory benefits. Alternative methods lead to a lower baseline (2005–2007) level of statutory after-tax wage replacement under S.B. 899. The constant-maturity DEU sample, which uses data on earnings losses and benefits for the same individuals, yields estimated after-tax wage replacement rates over the 2005–2012 period around 50 percent, as do our estimates using the WCIS that do not reweight the fraction of represented cases.

Table 5.4
After-Tax Wage Replacement Rates Under S.B. 899 and S.B. 863, by Year of Injury

	Injury Years 2005–2007 (%)	Injury Years 2008–2009 (%)	Injury Years 2010–2012 (%)	All Years (%)
S.B. 899 Benefits	64.3	57.1	52.4	58.8
S.B. 863 Maximum Applied to S.B. 899 Ratings	76.3	66.8	61.2	69.2
S.B. 863 Benefits and Ratings	85.4	74.3	66.4	76.8
S.B. 863 + Return to Work Fund	89.0	77.6	69.8	80.2

However, there are good reasons why we might expect these alternative methods to yield lower wage replacement rates, and so the differences in results do not necessarily indicate that the wage replacement estimates reported in this chapter are too high. A constant-maturity sample from the DEU systematically omits the most severe cases, which (as we discuss in Chapter Six) tend to have higher wage replacement rates over the fixed five-year time horizon we consider in this study. Similarly, estimates of benefits that do not account for the DEU's underrepresentation of cases with attorney involvement may lead to underestimates of replacement rates because cases with legal representation have higher ratings and benefits. The 50-percent figure may be a lower bound for the statutory after-tax wage replacement rate under S.B. 899.

More importantly, all these methods yield similar estimates of the change in benefit adequacy for the years 2005–2012, and of the influence of changes enacted under S.B. 863 on benefit adequacy: S.B. 863 would have increased after-tax wage replacement rates by 20 to 25 percentage points for the average worker injured during the 2005–2012 period (or 16 to 20 percentage points for the average worker injured in 2010–2012). We conclude that the large reductions in post-injury earnings that followed the Great Recession drove the trends in wage replacement rates. While alternative assumptions lead to higher estimated levels of statutory wage replacement, differences in the methodology used to estimate average statutory benefits do not alter the basic conclusion that after-tax wage replacement rates fell after the Great Recession, and that the benefit increases in S.B. 863 are large enough to offset these increases in earnings loss.

Potential Effects of *Almaraz v Guzman*

The above analysis did not incorporate the possible influence of the *Almaraz/Guzman* decisions. In order to illustrate how *Almaraz* could alter our findings, we present the first detailed estimates of the effect of *Almaraz/Guzman* using data from all DEU ratings under the AMA *Guides* performed between January 1 and May 13, 2016. This effort required key assistance from the DWC and especially the DEU to correctly identify how these ratings were handled by the DEU.

We find that *Almaraz* is likely to have had an important and substantial influence on the ratings and statutory benefits available to permanently disabled workers. We estimate the effect of an *Almaraz* rating relative to the underlying AMA rating. The estimated effect is given in Table 5.5. The average effect by type of rating is given at the top of the table (+ 9.7 rating points for Summary ratings, + 13.5 rating points for Consult ratings, and + 13.0 rating points for Formal ratings).

It is quite interesting and useful that the average effect of *Almaraz*, within rating type, is reasonably consistent across the range of underlying AMA ratings. Even when the underlying AMA rating is 0 percent or the rating is above 60 percent, the effect of *Almaraz* in absolute rating points is similar.

We have calculated the effect of alternative ratings on statutory benefits. Here we are estimating the effect if the alternative rating was used instead of the baseline AMA rating.

The estimates in Table 5.6 reflect the potentially large impact of alternative ratings among cases for which these ratings are calculated. These increases are large enough, and alternative ratings are widespread enough, that these ratings could have a meaningful influence on the average level of statutory benefits for all PPD cases. If all the alternative ratings performed by the DEU between 2012 and May 2015 (regardless of injury date) were legally valid, these ratings would increase statutory benefits for the average Summary-rated case by $1,300, or about

Table 5.5
Effect of *Almaraz/Guzman* on Final Ratings Before Apportionment

AMA Rating	Summary Ratings (Before Apportionment)				Consult Ratings (Before Apportionment)				Formal Ratings (Before Apportionment)			
	n =	Average AMA Rating	Average *Almaraz* Increase (%)	Standard Error of *Almaraz* Increase	n =	Average AMA Rating	Average *Almaraz* Increase (%)	Std. Err of *Almaraz* Increase	n =	Average AMA Rating	Average *Almaraz* Increase (%)	Std. Err of *Almaraz* Increase
All	1,743	9.59	9.71	0.202	8,574	23.10	13.48	0.127	38	34.08	13.00	1.77
0%	563	0.00	8.21	0.313	698	0.00	17.77	0.651				
1%–5%	293	3.28	9.60	0.451	644	3.32	13.02	0.435				
6%–10%	301	7.93	9.70	0.455	1,016	8.14	13.19	0.380				
11%–20%	338	15.29	11.00	0.550	2,231	15.55	13.51	0.239				
21%–40%	197	28.63	11.58	0.686	2,567	29.01	13.69	0.218				
41%–60%	47	47.91	11.26	0.949	1,014	48.50	12.61	0.318				
61%–99%	4	75.25	12.50	2.598	392	71.80	10.31	0.373				

NOTE: Data is from the DEU ratings for the period January 1 to May 13, 2015, under the AMA *Guides*–based PDRS.

Table 5.6
Estimated Effect of *Almaraz*-Type Ratings on PD Indemnity (cases with alternative ratings only, DEU ratings data, 2005–2015)

	Rating Type		
	Summary	Consult	Formal
AMA *Guides* Ratings	$13,089	$27,899	$47,425
Almaraz Ratings	$19,845	$47,192	$73,458
Difference ($)	$6,756	$19,293	$26,033
Difference (% of AMA)	51.6	69.2	54.9

10 percent. On Consults the increase would be about $4,800, or 17 percent. Formal ratings have a similar range of effects, but the small number of Formal ratings with information on both *Almaraz* and AMA ratings makes these estimates more unreliable.

The most important limitation of this analysis is that whether the AMA or *Almaraz* rating will ultimately prevail and be determinant of the amount of indemnity received by the worker involves two complex issues that are not visible in the DEU data.

The question of whether the doctor's report on the issue constitutes "substantial evidence" adequately setting forth the facts and reasoning for an alternative rating is a legal matter. That decision can only be made by a judge, who likely will choose one or the other rating as dispositive. It is also possible that the parties to the case can settle the issue without a legal finding. Under these circumstances, we would expect the settled amount of indemnity to fall somewhere between the levels of statutory benefits defined by the AMA *Guides* and *Almaraz* ratings. Consequently, the alternative rating should be seen as an upper bound on the effect of the *Almaraz/ Guzman* approach on the final rating in cases where an alternative rating is given.

Discussion

While statutory benefits trended upward over the 2005–2012 period, reduced earnings for injured workers outweighed the effect of higher benefits and led to a decline in after-tax wage replacement rates for workers injured in 2008 and later years. After-tax replacement rates for injuries in 2005–2007 were 64.3 percent for the WCIS, but fell to 52.4 percent for injuries in 2010–2012. Alternative methods lead to lower estimates of wage replacement rates but yield very similar trajectories of percentage-point declines over the 2005–2012 period.

A limitation of the method used to calculate after-tax replacement rates in this analysis is that we have included earnings losses in the first post-injury year in the denominator of our wage replacement rates. A portion of earnings losses during the first post-injury year is likely to include lost earnings that were compensated by temporary total disability benefits, and so our estimates may overstate the level of earnings losses experienced over the first five years *of permanent disability*: the median duration between the date of injury and the date of maximum medical improvement in the WCIS is slightly over one year, meaning that this would be a concern for the typical worker. An alternative approach that is less likely to capture losses due to temporary total disability is to calculate earnings losses over the second through fifth post-injury years and scale up the result by 25 percent to approximate losses over the first five years of the permanent disability period. This method would reduce our estimates of five-year earnings loss by 4.9 percent across the board, implying 2005–2012 average after-tax wage replacement rates under S.B. 899 that are 3 percentage points higher than those reported in Table 5.4, but not meaningfully changing our conclusions about how replacement rates evolved over time or the influence of S.B. 863. We do not view this as a major limitation of our analysis, since (as discussed above) the choice of a five-year wage window over which to evaluate benefit adequacy is likely to understate lifetime earnings losses for most workers.

Our estimates suggest that S.B. 863 led to a dramatic improvement in the adequacy of PPD benefits as the S.B. 863 reforms were phased in during 2012–2014. The increases in benefits and ratings due to S.B. 863 were substantial enough to undo the effects of higher earnings losses and increase wage replacement rates slightly above the levels observed in 2005–2007 under S.B. 899. For injuries occurring in 2010–2012, estimated after-tax replacement rates under the S.B. 863 benefit and rating changes would have been 69.8 percent for the WCIS, significantly higher than the 52.4-percent replacement rate under S.B. 899. The most important factor explaining declining replacement rates over this period appears to be increased earnings losses during the Great Recession. Because earnings fell so sharply, much of the increase in benefits enacted under S.B. 863 serves to return replacement rates to approximately the level (64.3 percent) observed under S.B. 899 for the period prior to the recession.

CHAPTER SIX

Effects of S.B. 863 on Disability Ratings and Benefit Equity

In addition to overall benefit adequacy, a fair assignment of benefits to workers should also be a policy objective of the workers' compensation system. In this chapter, we analyze the implications of S.B. 863 for the fairness, or *equity*, of PD ratings and indemnity benefits. S.B. 863, as discussed in Chapter Five, will substantially increase overall wage replacement rates for permanently disabled workers, offsetting the declines in post-injury earnings documented in Chapter Four. However, there is no guarantee that improvements in adequacy will simultaneously improve the equity of the rating and benefit systems across different groups of workers, or that increase in benefits will be targeted to the workers experiencing the greatest losses.

This chapter considers the provisions of S.B. 863 and examines detailed data on disability ratings conducted under S.B. 899 and under S.B. 863 to address the following questions:

- What influences would we expect S.B. 863 to have on the equity of PD ratings and benefits?
- Has S.B. 863 affected the initial ratings performed under the new rating system?
- What was the relationship between earnings losses, ratings, and benefits under S.B. 899 for the average impairment, and how will S.B. 863 change this relationship?
- How were different impairments of similar severity treated under S.B. 899, and what will be the effects of S.B. 863?
- Will S.B. 863 affect low-wage and high-wage workers differently?

Which Groups of Disabled Workers Will Be Affected by Rating and Benefits Changes Under S.B. 863?

S.B. 863 made a number of changes to the calculation of ratings and the rate at which PPD benefits are paid. First, the legislation eliminated compensation for certain secondary impairments that were "added on" to the primary impairment. These included sleep, sexual dysfunction, and psychiatric impairments secondary to a primary condition. Sleep and sexual dysfunction had very small effects on overall average ratings, but psychiatric impairments were expected to have an important effect.

Second, S.B. 863 eliminated the 15-percent bump up/bump down in the weekly PPD benefit rate that depended on whether the at-injury employer could offer a worker post-injury employment with a wage near pre-injury levels. If the employer offered such work, weekly benefits were reduced by 15 percent. If no complying offer was made, benefits were increased by 15 percent. Like the add-on elimination, the bump-up/bump-down elimination was expected to have limited effect because the implementing language in S.B. 899 was interpreted by the courts to mean a substantial fraction of PPD benefits are paid out before the bump up/bump down could be applied.

S.B. 863 also increased all FEC adjustment factors to 1.4. Under S.B. 899, FEC factors ranged from 1.1 to 1.4 and averaged 1.22. This was expected to lead to a substantial increase in PPD indemnity, but also to vary substantially by the type of impairment. For example, impairments of the hand/fingers would have their FEC increased from 1.1 to 1.4. Psychiatric impairments would have the same FEC (1.4) under S.B. 899 and S.B. 863.

In short, changes in disability ratings under S.B. 863 will primarily affect workers whose impairments are from lower FEC groups. As discussed in Chapter Five, much of the increase in benefits under S.B. 863 will come about through the increase in the maximum weekly wage used in calculating PPD benefits and, to a lesser extent, the increase in the minimum weekly wage. These increases should have the largest effect on workers with wages above the weekly maximum wage under S.B. 899. The return to work benefit will have a more limited effect on adequacy because it is fixed at a fairly modest amount independently of the worker's earnings, but this design feature should make it more valuable to lower-wage workers, while the fact that the return to work benefit is tied to post-injury outcomes (in contrast to other PPD benefits) could allow it to have a larger effect on the equity of benefits.

In the remainder of this chapter, we present analyses of how the rating changes under S.B. 863 are likely to affect the distribution of impairment ratings and the fairness of the disability rating system. As in Chapter Five, the limited amount of data on ratings actually conducted under S.B. 863 leads us to focus instead on simulating outcomes for the population of cases rated under S.B. 899. We focus exclusively on cases evaluated at the DEU in this chapter because evaluation of equity requires detailed information about the specific impairments that affect each worker.

DEU Rating Data

Table 6.1 presents summary statistics on cases rated at the DEU under S.B. 899 through May 2015. Our analysis sample for this table excludes cases with incomplete information on final ratings, impairment codes, or the type of rating, but includes cases that were not matched to earnings data from EDD. These exclusions leave us with 191,477 unique cases from injuries occurring between 2005 and 2012. In contrast to Chapter Five, where we focused on a constant-maturity sample of DEU cases in order to analyze trends in ratings, in Table 6.1 and the subsequent analysis, we use all available ratings regardless of case. Pooling all these cases together, the average final rating before apportionment was 20.3. At the statutory maximum wage under S.B. 899, nominal statutory benefits averaged $21,432, excluding life pensions, and $23,098, including the present discounted value of life pensions.[1] A single rated impairment was identified in 65.4 percent of cases, with 19.0 percent having two rated impairments, and 15.6 percent having three or more rated impairments.

---

[1]   Conversion of life pensions into a present value is complicated because the life span of a beneficiary is uncertain. We assume that life pensions are received as a lump sum as soon as the worker becomes eligible for payments to begin, but we discount this lump sum back to the date of injury at a 2.3-percent discount rate. We also assume that workers live to age 80.

Table 6.2
Body System Distribution and Add-on Impairments Among DEU Ratings Performed Under S.B. 899

	All Ratings	Consult Ratings	Summary Ratings	Formal
Body System of Highest-Rated Impairment (%)				
Spine	36.8	42.4	29.4	42.3
Upper	32.1	26.2	40.1	17.3
Lower	17.8	13.3	23.7	9.0
Mental/Behavioral	4.9	7.3	1.7	11.2
Central/Peripheral Nervous System	2.4	3.5	1.0	4.5
Cardiovascular (Any)	1.9	2.4	1.0	7.4
Digestive	1.3	1.9	0.4	3.4
Other	2.9	3.1	2.6	4.6
Percentage with Add-on Impairments				
Psychiatric	2.2	3.7	0.2	5.9
Sleep Disorder	0.6	0.9	0.1	2.6
Sexual Dysfunction	0.1	0.2	0.1	0.5
Pain	16.3	22.5	8.5	19.6

NOTE: Sample includes all DEU cases with injury date during 2005–2012 with final rating reported, impairment code for highest-rated impairment, and rating type (Consult, Summary, or Formal) reported.

were eliminated by S.B. 863 for injuries occurring in 2013 and later years. Table 6.2 shows these add-ons were used somewhat rarely, with psychiatric add-ons being the most commonly used (2.2 percent of all cases), followed by sleep disorders (0.57 percent of cases) and sexual dysfunction (0.14 percent of all cases). While infrequent, sleep and psychiatric add-ons had been increasing steadily over the 2005–2012 period. The pain add-on, in contrast, appears on 16.4 percent of all cases. The second through fourth columns show that the eliminated add-ons were used almost entirely in represented (Consult) ratings and Formal ratings, and almost never in Summary ratings.

Early Impairment Ratings Under S.B. 863

Table 6.3 compares early ratings for the last injuries to occur under S.B. 899 to the first injuries to occur under S.B. 863. We examine injuries occurring in 2012 and 2013 and restrict attention to a constant-maturity subpopulation of injuries rated at the DEU within 486 days of injury. This is the highest maturity at which 2013 injuries can be compared to earlier years without inducing bias due to right-truncation. We present statistics for all rating types pooled together.

Among this constant-maturity subpopulation of cases, the distribution of injury type and severity did not change between 2013 and 2014. The average combined standard rating was 9.1 for 2012 injuries and 9.2 for 2013 injuries, but this difference was both small in practical terms and statistically insignificant (p = 0.59). The average number of rated impairments (1.4) remained constant across both years. Moreover, the distribution of cases by body system of

Table 6.3
Early Effects of S.B. 863 on DEU Ratings

Injury Year	2013 Comparable Constant Maturity		Statistically Significant Difference?
	2012	2013	
S.B. 863 in Effect?	No	Yes	
Combined Standard Rating (WPI)	9.1	9.2	
Number of Impairments	1.4	1.4	
Body System of Highest-Rated Impairment			
Spine	33.61	33.99	
Upper	34.80	34.12	
Lower	19.69	19.34	
Mental/Behavioral	3.78	3.83	
Central/Peripheral Nervous System	1.65	1.45	
Cardiovascular (Any)	2.00	2.69	
Digestive	1.02	0.95	
Other	3.45	3.62	
Percentage of Consult Ratings	33.63	41.40	***
Percentage with Add-on Impairments			
Psychiatric	0.47	0.36	
Sleep Disorder	0.24	0.04	**
Sexual Dysfunction	0.02	0.02	
Pain	14.80	15.85	
Final Rating Before Apportionment*	15.1	16.9	***
Statutory Benefit at Maximum Weekly Wage			
Without Life Pension	$14,350	$17,116	***
Including Life Pension*	$15,103	$17,771	***
Number of Cases	5,103	4,751	
Days to First Rating			
Average	340	346	
Median	354	357	

* p < 0.1, ** p < 0.05, *** p < 0.01
NOTES: Significance assessed using unequal variance t-tests for continuous variables and chi-squared tests for binary and categorical variables. Sample contains cases rated within 486 days of injury.

primary impairment was statistically identical across years (p = 0.47). These statistics provide strong evidence that, among low-maturity cases, the severity and type of impairments among the population of injured workers evaluated at the DEU did not change with implementation of S.B. 863. This is somewhat surprising in light of the fact that there was a statistically significant increase of 7.8 percentage points in the share of Consult ratings following implementation of S.B. 863, since we have seen that Consult ratings tend to be more severe cases and have a different distribution of impairments.[2] It appears, however, that restriction to a constant-maturity subpopulation outweighs the influence of these changes in representation status: it is quite likely that higher-maturity cases are responsible for the overall compositional differences between Consult and Summary ratings.

While the type and severity of injuries remained constant for low-maturity claims through enactment of S.B. 863, changes to the rating system and benefit schedule have had the antici-pated effects of increasing final ratings and statutory benefits. The average final rating before apportionment increased by 1.8 percentage points, from 15.1 percent to 16.9 percent.

Surprisingly, psychiatric add-ons restricted under S.B. 899 continue to appear under S.B. 863. The sleep disorder add-on and the sexual dysfunction add-on are used in just a hand-ful of cases after S.B. 863. However, these add-ons were also rare among low-maturity cases under S.B. 899. For example, Table 6.1 showed that 2.2 percent of the overall population of S.B. 899 ratings had psychiatric add-ons, as compared to just 0.5 percent among the constant-maturity subpopulation examined in Table 6.3. The early data under S.B. 863 therefore sug-gest that restriction of the add-ons had a trivial effect on ratings that was far outweighed by the increases to FEC, but the available data do not capture the high-severity cases where we might expect to see a larger effect of the add-on restrictions.

The far more common pain add-on appears on slightly more cases after implementation of S.B. 863 (15.9 percent versus 14.8 percent), but this difference is not statistically significant at conventional levels ($p = 0.16$). This appears to reflect the higher share of represented ratings rather than a change in the rating process, as differences between 2013 and 2012 in the frac-tion of cases with pain add-ons are statistically insignificant (though slightly positive) after stratifying on rating type.

The net effect of the changes to ratings, along with the increase in the maximum weekly wage used to calculate benefits, was to substantially increase statutory benefits for low-maturity cases. The average statutory benefit for injuries in our low-maturity subpopulation was $14,350 ($15,103 including life pensions) for 2012 and $17,116 ($17,771 including life pensions) for 2013, representing an increase in benefits of 19 percent (18 percent including life pensions).

These increases are substantially lower than the increases reported in Chapter Five, but this is simply a mechanical consequence of the truncation of our sample at such a low point of the maturity distribution. As depicted in Figure 6.1, less than a quarter of cases from a typi-cal injury cohort reach the DEU within 486 days of injury. As depicted in Figure 6.2 and

---

[2]   We cannot offer a definitive explanation for the increased share of cases with representation after implementation of S.B. 863, but there are several interesting possibilities. One possibility is that workers needed more guidance to navigate the workers' compensation system after implementation of S.B. 863 and became more likely to seek out representation. How-ever, another possibility is that some cases where the date of injury is subject to ambiguity—for instance, cumulative injury claims or post-termination claims—were shifted from 2012 injury dates to 2013 injury dates because the increases in benefits under S.B. 863 create an incentive to shift claims into 2013. The increase in the share of Consult ratings in 2013 is consistent with a scenario in which attorneys (who have a better understanding of the incentives built into the workers' compensation system than applicants) might advise clients to shift injury dates forward when there is ambiguity, but that unrepresented workers may be less aware of these incentives.

In an analysis not reported in this study, we found suggestive evidence that the volume of Consult ratings exhibited a trend break following implementation of S.B. 863, and that this effect may have been more pronounced for cumulative injuries than for non-cumulative injuries. However, we consider these findings merely suggestive, as statistical tests for the hypothesis that injuries were shifted from late 2012 to early 2013 do not yield strong support for this proposition after controlling for seasonality in the volume of injuries. The more pronounced increase in Consult ratings occurs later in 2013, whereas one might expect shifting injury dates to result in a spike of cases early in 2013.

Figure 6.3, these are the least severe injuries in the injury cohort. These facts mean that we will not be able to infer the full influence of S.B. 863 on ratings or benefits by examining ratings actually performed under S.B. 863 until several more years have passed.

Equity in Permanent Disability Ratings and Benefits

At present, we can only observe a severely truncated sample of ratings actually performed under S.B. 863. Chapter Five presented analyses of trends in benefit adequacy and replacement rates under S.B. 863 that addressed the right-truncation problems created by the lag between injuries and DEU ratings by combining wage loss data from the WCIS with trends in benefits estimated using high-maturity cases from the DEU. In order to evaluate how the changes to benefits and ratings under S.B. 863 will affect the equity of PPD benefits, we abstract from time trends and pool together all ratings performed to date under S.B. 899. Our analysis of equity should therefore be interpreted as capturing outcomes for an average injury within a group being measured occurring between 2005 and 2012 that was rated by May 2015.

We follow previous RAND studies in distinguishing between two dimensions along which the fairness, or equity, of the disability rating system can be evaluated: vertical equity and horizontal equity (Peterson et al., 1998; Reville, Seabury, et al., 2005; Bhattacharya et al., 2010). *Vertical equity* refers to the principle that workers with more severe earnings losses should receive proportionally more generous benefits to offset those losses. *Horizontal equity* refers to the principle that similarly situated workers should be treated similarly.

We also examine how S.B. 863 affects the *progressivity* of benefits, which we define as the extent to which the wage replacement rate is higher for lower-wage workers. While the appropriateness of progressivity as a policy objective for the workers' compensation system (as opposed to tax policy and other social insurance) is debatable, the use of minimum and maximum weekly wage amounts in calculating PPD benefits introduces a considerable degree of progressivity into workers' compensation benefits in California and other jurisdictions.[3] Because increases in benefits under S.B. 863 are accomplished in large part by increasing the weekly maximum benefit, stakeholders may find it of interest to examine the effects of the reforms across the income distribution. This may be particularly true in light of our finding in Chapter Four that low-wage workers experience larger proportional earnings losses than otherwise identical high-wage workers.

As in past RAND work, we evaluate the equity of ratings and benefits by measuring the relationship between ratings and earnings losses. Because S.B. 863 involved important changes to benefits as well as changes to the rating system, we also examine the relationship between earnings losses and benefits by grouping together workers with similar ratings and then comparing benefits and earnings losses across these groups. Finally, we compare the progressivity of benefits under S.B. 899 and S.B. 863 by calculating wage replacement rates stratified on the worker's pre-injury wage.

---

[3]   Some authors have suggested that progressivity should be considered an element of vertical equity in evaluating the design of workers' compensation benefits (Gunderson and Hyatt, 1998). Gunderson and Hyatt also offer an informative discussion of the role of minimum and maximum benefits in creating progressivity.

the second and third quartiles of pre-injury earnings, and roughly equal to the after-tax wage replacement rates for workers in the highest quartile of pre-injury earnings. However, some might argue that the differential increases in after-tax wage replacement rates in the second quartile of pre-injury earnings (compared with higher earnings levels) represents an increase in progressivity, and we do not take a stand on the optimal degree of progressivity for PPD benefits.

Compared with the benefit and ratings changes under S.B. 863, the effects of the return to work benefit on after-tax wage replacement rates across the income distribution are markedly different. Relative to replacement rates under the other ratings and benefit provisions of S.B. 863, our estimates suggest that the return to work benefit could increase wage replacement rates for workers in the first quartile of pre-injury annual earnings by as much as 14 percentage points. The incremental effects of the return to work benefit on replacement rates fall sharply with pre-injury earnings, to 7 percentage points in the second quartile, 4 percentage points in the third quartile, and 2 percentage points in the fourth quartile. Although these estimates are likely to represent an upper bound on eligibility for the return to work benefit, we do not believe that our measure of return to work fund eligibility overstates or understates eligibility in a way that is correlated with the worker's pre-injury wage.[11] The feature of the return to work benefit that limited its effect on vertical equity—namely its fixed dollar value regardless of pre-injury wages—appears to make it strongly progressive.

Horizontal Equity

The provision of S.B. 863 most likely to affect horizontal equity is the elimination of differences between impairment types in the FEC adjustment. As discussed above, increases in final ratings and benefits due to setting the FEC to 1.4 for all impairments may be inversely related to the pattern of earnings losses across impairments with similar standard ratings. While our analysis of vertical equity showed that the changes to the rating system differentially affected cases with low earnings losses, resulting changes in the relationship between earnings losses and benefits were offset by the increase in the weekly maximum and the shape of the overall relationship between earnings losses and benefits is similar under S.B. 863 and S.B. 899. We might expect to see larger effects of S.B. 863 on horizontal equity. In particular, we may be concerned that horizontal inequities across impairments in different FEC groupings could be exacerbated rather than reduced.

We examined this possibility by comparing proportional earnings losses for cases with similar ratings across different impairment types, which replicates methods used to examine horizontal equity in prior RAND reports. Our graphical analysis focuses on seven impairments chosen to span the range of FEC groups.[12] These are defined in Table 6.6, which also presents the average impairment ratings and earnings loss for these impairments. Table 6.6 makes it clear that there are substantial differences in both ratings and earnings losses across these impairment groups, which is why it is important to stratify on ratings when examining horizontal equity. To isolate the effect of changes in the FEC factors, we restrict attention to single-impairment cases and use ratings before apportionment.

---

[11] See Appendix D for discussion.

[12] FEC rank 3 is rarely used, and there was an insufficient number of cases available for our analysis.

Table 6.6
Selected Impairments for Horizontal Equity Analysis

FEC Group	Impairment Name	Impairment Number	Number of Cases 2005–2012	S.B. 899 Final Rating Before Apportionment	S.B. 863 Final Rating Before Apportionment	Relative Earnings, Second Post-Injury Year (%)
1	Hand or finger impairment	16.05.xx.xx or 16.06.xx.xx	6,137	6.0	7.6	95.1
2	Knee impairment	17.05.xx.xx	14,667	8.4	10.1	89.2
4	Carpal tunnel syndrome	16.01.02.02	1,766	7.1	8.0	86.0
5	Low back pain	15.03.01.00 or 15.03.02.02	18,422	15.2	16.7	72.9
6	Digestive system impairment	06.xx.00.xx	371	17.9	18.9	64.8
7	Shoulder impairment	16.02.01.xx or 16.02.02.xx	13,901	11.0	11.3	81.6
8	Psychiatric impairment	14.01.00.00	3,330	26.0	26.1	46.2

Figure 6.8 depicts the horizontal equity of final ratings under S.B. 899 for these impairments. Each cluster of bars represents the population of cases with ratings in a given range; for instance, the first seven bars represent cases with final ratings between 0 and 4.75. The bars are ordered by FEC group. If the rating system were completely accurate in predicting proportional earnings losses (and thus in targeting benefits to earnings losses), we would expect all the bars at each rating level to have the same height. Instead, we find some systematic differences between similarly rated cases with different impairments. These differences are most apparent among ratings below 30, which is the range that most cases rated at the DEU fall into. (While the average final rating before apportionment for 2005–2012 injuries in our DEU population is 20.3, the median final rating was 15, and 75 percent of cases received ratings of 28 or lower.)

As observed in previous RAND studies, earnings losses are extremely high among cases with psychiatric impairments, even at the bottom of the rating distribution.[13] The relationship between earnings losses and ratings is nearly identical between S.B. 863 and S.B. 899, which is in line with our expectations given that psychiatric impairments are not affected by changes to the FEC under S.B. 863. Because S.B. 863 pushes cases with less severe earnings losses up the rating distribution, however, horizontal equity between psychiatric cases and other impairments appears to worsen under S.B. 863.

Note that these ratings incorporate the FEC adjustment as set under S.B. 899. The fact that, within each rating group, losses remain lower for impairments in the lowest FEC groups—a pattern reflected in Figure 6.8 by the increasing height of bars from top to bottom

---

[13] The pre–2005 PDRS used a series of measures for calculating the percent disability for a psychiatric impairment rating. These measures were idiosyncratic to California's rating system. The fifth edition of the AMA *Guides* adopted under S.B. 899 did not include a method for measuring psychiatric impairment. Thus California adopted the GAF measurement system, which had been in wide use and validated under limited testing. Subsequently, the AMA adopted the GAF for the sixth edition of the *Guides*. Interestingly, while the pre–2005 California approach was shown in earlier RAND studies to be a very poor predictor of the economic consequences of a psychiatric disability, the GAF, while a very different measurement system, appears to show little, if any, improvement at predicting earnings loss.

CHAPTER SEVEN

Conclusions and Policy Recommendations

Overview of Key Findings

In this study we examined recent trends in the economic outcomes of permanently disabled workers in the California workers' compensation system and the potential effect of the permanent disability benefit increases enacted in S.B. 863. We estimated the level of earnings losses experienced by permanently disabled workers injured between 2005 and 2012, and compared the compensation that was offered to these workers to what would have been offered had the new reforms been in place. We also examined several other recent legislative, judicial, and regulatory changes in the workers' compensation system and their implications for the adequacy and equity of benefits. Our central findings included the following:

- Permanently disabled workers injured after the beginning of the Great Recession experienced much more severe earnings losses than workers injured before, suggesting that the economic downturn disproportionately affected injured workers relative to uninjured workers.

- For the average worker who was injured between 2005 and 2012, the benefit increases enacted under S.B. 863 would have significantly increased replacement rates of lost income compared to what they were under S.B. 899. Specifically, we estimated that the fraction of after-tax earnings losses replaced by benefits would have risen by 21.4 percentage points, from 58.8 percent to 80.2 percent.

- While S.B. 863 has led to higher PPD benefits, future trends in the replacement rate of lost earnings will be driven in large part by the extent to which earnings of disabled workers recover from the Great Recession.

- Both changes in ratings and increases in the maximum weekly wage led to substantial increases in benefit adequacy, while the return to work benefit had a more modest effect on average. However, the return to work benefit has the largest effect on wage replacement rates for the lowest-wage workers. Since the other provisions of S.B. 863 lead to larger benefit increases for middle-income and high-income workers, the return to work benefit has an important role to play in preserving the progressivity of PPD benefits.

- The elimination of the FEC adjustment had little effect on the overall equity of disability benefits across workers with different types of injuries. This is largely due to the fact that the FEC as implemented was based on the old California PDRS and did little to address discrepancies in the relationship between earnings losses and disability ratings under the AMA *Guides*.

- In addition to future economic trends, two of the biggest uncertainties regarding future trends in PPD benefits are the use of alternative disability rating procedures based on the *Almaraz* decision and the take-up of the return to work benefit. These and other system factors require careful monitoring by CHSWC and other policymakers and stakeholders.

These findings have many important policy implications for permanent partial disability compensation in California, which we discuss in detail over the remainder of this chapter.

The Role of Economic Conditions in Assessing Benefit Adequacy

In Chapter Four we documented that the economic outcomes of permanently disabled workers worsened considerably during the Great Recession, with relatively little improvement through the end of 2012. The gap between the earnings of injured workers and control workers increased rapidly after the onset of the recession, leading to a dramatic increase in average earnings loss for injured workers.

A number of factors could potentially lead to greater earnings losses during periods of economic hardship. We found that a large portion of the increase in earnings loss associated with the recession was actually due to changes in the types of workers claiming PPD benefits. That is, in the wake of the recession, the population of permanently disabled workers shifted toward groups of workers that tend to experience larger earnings losses. For example, compared to the average worker with a PPD claim injured during 2005–2007, workers injured in 2008 and later were older, had more severe injuries, and had lower pre-injury earnings. There are many possible explanations as to why the composition of the population of PPD claimants may have changed. For example, it is possible that workers with less severe injuries are less likely to file for PPD benefits when economic conditions are poor because they fear employer retribution and don't want to lose their job. Ultimately, our data do not allow us to identify the cause of compositional changes, but this is an important issue for future research to identify and address.

While compositional changes drove a large part of the trend in earnings losses, we nonetheless witnessed a significant increase in earnings loss even when we used more advanced statistical methods to control for the changes in composition. This finding can be illustrated by imagining two identical workers (with the same job, demographics, and wage) who experienced the same injury at different points in time. If one of these workers was injured before the recession (say, in 2005) and the other had been injured after the recession (say, in 2012) the worker injured after the recession would have experienced much greater earnings loss. This suggests that worsening economic conditions put disabled workers even more at risk than they were under times of prosperity such as the mid–2000s.

From a policy perspective, the effect of the business cycle on earnings losses may provide an additional rationale for targeting benefits toward more vulnerable groups. In California, PPD benefits are designed to vary according to the severity of injury but not underlying economic conditions. Thus, the measured adequacy of benefits will vary according to the earnings losses experienced by disabled workers, so when economic conditions worsen and earnings losses rise, benefit adequacy falls. Policymakers could help stabilize benefit adequacy through economic upswings and downswings by designing benefits that lead to similar wage replacement rates across different populations of workers. One such targeting mechanism that has been suggested by past work is the tying of benefit levels to offers of return to work (Reville, Seabury, et al., 2005; Seabury et al., 2011).

From the perspective of targeting benefits according to expected earnings losses, S.B. 863 was arguably mixed. The tiered benefit introduced by S.B. 899—the "bump up, bump down"—was designed to promote return to work by offering higher benefits when no return to work offer was made and lower benefits when such an offer was extended. However, there were problems with the implementation of this policy and concern over the costs of administering it (Seabury et al., 2011), and it was eliminated by S.B. 863. The new reform did provide some targeting of benefits to vulnerable populations of workers through the return to work fund, though the size of the benefit is too small to materially affect the wage replacement rate for the average worker.

Future study should explore benefit design options that minimize administrative complications but do more to smooth out the kind of fluctuations in wage replacement across the business cycle that we identified in this report. Policymakers considering how benefit design could be made more responsive to the business cycle should, however, think carefully about the financing of any such benefits, as policies that would necessitate premium increases while the labor market is slack could in theory lead to adverse effects on hiring.

Other Factors That Influence Long-Run Benefit Adequacy

The benefit increases introduced by S.B. 863 significantly increased the adequacy of PPD benefits in California, more than making up for the declines in PD ratings that followed adoption of the AMA *Guides* under S.B. 899. This is despite the fact that earnings losses increased significantly in the wake of the Great Recession. Going forward, if the economy continues to improve and earnings losses fall we expect that benefit adequacy would further rise, to the extent that after-tax replacement rates could exceed 80 percent. However, there are several factors that make it difficult to forecast future replacement rates. One is a general point that while the economy has been improving, there is uncertainty about future economic growth. Additionally, even if the economy does improve, there could be future downward pressure on replacement rates if an improving economy leads to wage inflation.

As in most states, weekly cash benefits in California—temporary and permanent—are equal to two-thirds of pre-injury wages subject to fixed minimums and maximums. As we discussed in Chapter Five, unlike the TTD maximum, California's PPD weekly maximum benefit is fixed by statute and not adjusted for changes in wage growth or inflation. Accordingly, real benefits and effective replacement rates tend to erode over time due to inflation and real wage growth.

The fixed nature of the maximum weekly wage has significant implications for trends in benefit adequacy. Under S.B. 863, the maximum weekly PPD benefit applicable to most cases increased by 26 percent in 2014. However, this was the first increase in the maximum benefit since 2006, and the real value of the maximum benefit declined by 13 percent between 2006 and 2014 due to inflation. The new maximum benefit under S.B. 863 is only 7 percent higher than the real value of the previous maximum benefit in 2006. In other words, the majority of the increase in benefit adequacy resulting from the new maximum was necessary to offset the decline in real benefit levels brought about by inflation. If the economic recovery continues and it leads to real wage growth, this could cause the level of earnings losses to rise faster than benefits and lower replacement rates in the future.

A simple way to address the potential erosion of replacement rates over time is to index PPD benefits to inflation the same way that TTD benefits are. However, indexation of PPD benefits is not particularly common in the United States. We examined the U.S. Chamber of Commerce *Analysis of Workers' Compensation Laws* to learn how other states handle indexation of the PPD benefit maximum. As of 2012, just 18 states indexed the maximum wage for computing PPD benefits to the state average wage.[1] If PPD benefits are to be fixed in nominal terms, it further reinforces the need to carefully monitor the adequacy of benefits to ensure that replacement rates do not become too high or too low as underlying economic fundamentals evolve.

The Equity of Permanent Disability Benefits

The impairment rating system and the benefit schedule are the policy instruments for determining an individual claimant's PPD benefits, and ideally they should allocate benefits in a fair and cost-effective manner. Vertical equity, defined as the property of assigning higher ratings and benefits to workers with more severe losses, is a fundamental normative principle for the design of workers' compensation benefits. We found that the AMA *Guides* ratings were quite successful at predicting the severity of work disability and earnings losses that are likely to result from a given impairment.[2] On a foundational level, then, California's current approach to determining disability benefits is consistent with vertical equity.

There was arguably more potential for S.B. 863 to negatively affect the PPD schedule's horizontal equity, defined as allocating benefits such that workers with similar losses receive similar benefits regardless of the type of injury. This is because the design of the FEC was, in principle, intended to help normalize the relationship between expected losses and average ratings across body part. If the FEC worked well, then eliminating it by fixing it to a single value could actually have worsened horizontal equity. However, while we found that there are significant differences in the compensation of injuries with similar earnings loss depending on the nature of injury, we found no evidence that these differences were exacerbated by S.B. 863. This suggests that the previous FECs probably did not do a particularly good job of promoting horizontal equity, likely because it was based on data from the old California rating system and not the AMA *Guides*.

This suggests that while S.B. 863 did not worsen horizontal equity, it also didn't improve it. Future research should consider whether the differences in the relationship between earnings losses and ratings across body parts could be alleviated.

---

[1]   The 18 states that indexed the maximum PPD benefit to the statewide average wage were Alabama, Arizona, Arkansas, Hawaii, Idaho, Kansas, Kentucky, Maryland, Missouri, Montana, New Jersey, New York, North Dakota, Ohio, Oregon, Rhode Island, Utah, and West Virginia (U.S. Chamber of Commerce, 2012).

[2]   This is consistent with the findings of Seabury and Scherer (2013).

Adjusting Benefits for Age and Occupation

Another way to target PPD benefits more accurately would be to modify the formula to convert *impairment* ratings to *disability* ratings according to differences in worker characteristics. In California, occupation and age are two dimensions that are currently used to adjust PPD benefits. These adjustments reflect beliefs about the interaction between age and occupation and a worker's underlying impairment that determines the degree of disability. The goals of these adjustments are to better match benefits to the expected effect of workers' impairments on future earnings.

The effect of the age and occupation adjustments under the current PDRS can be substantial. Table 7.1 illustrates the degree to which benefits paid for the same common impairment can be affected by a worker's occupation and age. The example is for a diagnosis-related estimate for lumbar category 3 with an AMA *Guides* WPI of 10 percent. A worker with neutral occupation and age adjustments (39-year-old medical technician) would receive a final rating of 14 percent and PPD benefits of $13,412 if earning at least $435/week. Depending on their age and occupation adjustments, workers with the same impairment and identical pre-injury wage could receive as little as $6,090 or as much as $35,742.

While this variation in benefits paid to different workers with similar impairments is intended to target workers with higher expected losses, it has never been empirically validated for equity or its effect on adequacy. In fact, prior work has questioned whether the reduction of benefits for younger workers actually matches the empirical patterns of earnings loss (Reville, Seabury, et al., 2005). Although the present study did not analyze occupation and age as factors affecting adequacy and equity, a reasonably straightforward modification to the methodology would allow the WCIS and DEU data to be used to much more precisely measure and predict the influence of age and occupation on future earnings loss. In turn, this would allow the occupation and age matrices in the PDRS to be redefined to improve equity and also as a tool to improve adequacy.

Labor Code 4660.1(e) sets the requirement that the "schedule of age and occupational modifiers shall promote consistency, uniformity, and objectivity." Future work should seek to

Table 7.1
Effect of Occupation and Age Adjustments Under California's PDRS

	Clerk, Aged 21	Medical Technician, Aged 39	Skilled Construction Worker, Aged 62
Impairment	Lower back	Lower back	Lower back
WPI (Standard rating) (%)	10	10	10
FEC	1.4	1.4	1.4
Rating (after FEC) (%)	14	14	14
Occupation group	110	310	420
Occupational Variant	C	F	J
Rating (after Occupation Adjustment) (%)	10	14	22
Final Rating (after Age Adjustment) (%)	7	14	29
PD benefits (at AWW > $435)	$6,090	$13,412	$35,742

NOTE: Examples based on California 2005 PDRS.

establish a consistent, objective- and empirically based system for incorporating these adjustments into the rating schedule.

Almaraz and Other Uncertainties

In this report, we focused primarily on changes to statute law and DIR regulations, such as the return to work fund. But the law is implemented by the courts and shaped by the behavior of lawyers, doctors, and other participants in the system. We identify some factors that DIR should monitor closely in order to keep track of potential further changes in equity, adequacy, and costs.

Almaraz ratings have diffused rapidly and are now performed on one in four cases rated at the DEU. S.B. 863 codified the *Almaraz/Guzman* series of WCAB en banc decisions. We estimate that the ratings calculated under the *Almaraz* approach are substantially higher than AMA ratings on the same cases and could lead to as much as an average $19,000 higher disability payments (69 percent) for represented workers getting an alternative rating. This would be about an average of $4,800 in additional benefits when spread across all represented workers. Unrepresented workers tend to get smaller percentage increases (52 percent) and smaller absolute increases ($6,800) when given an alternative rating. These are potentially very important increases to the benefits we calculate in this study for purposes of estimating adequacy. Compared to our estimates of statutory after-tax wage replacement under S.B. 863 for 2010–2012 injuries, *Almaraz* ratings could have increased wage replacement rates for 2010–2012 injuries by as much as 9.2 percentage points, from 61.1 percent to 70.3 percent. It is important to note that this large effect on benefit adequacy is an upper bound that assumes that all *Almaraz* ratings are legally valid, and so there is substantial uncertainty regarding the true effect of *Almaraz* ratings on statutory and paid benefits.

Departure from the AMA *Guides* warrants close scrutiny on vertical and horizontal equity grounds. *Almaraz* ratings are certain to increase overall compensation, but it isn't clear if that compensation increase is well targeted at those with disproportionate earnings losses. Horizontal equity may improve or degrade, depending on if *Almaraz* ratings systematically factor in information that is predictive of earnings losses or if they add greater variability and uncertainty but no additional precision.

The effects of *Almaraz* on equity are more difficult to evaluate empirically, however, for several reasons. It is unlikely that *Almaraz* ratings are assigned at random with respect to severity/complexity earnings losses. It is also possible that they lead to disputes, which could create reverse causation between ratings and expected earnings losses. Despite those challenges and because AMA *Guides* are widely used in other jurisdictions, it would be important and relatively straightforward to evaluate, on claims with both AMA and alternative *Almaraz* ratings, which of the two types of ratings more accurately predicted future wage loss. This would be a very valuable direction for future research on the California system.

We also suggest that DIR may wish to monitor WCAB rulings to see if the *Almaraz* ratings are holding up in court and, if possible, linking to WCIS to evaluate effect on paid amounts. Insurance data from WCIRB, SCIF, or others could also provide an important complementary data source to monitor how *Almaraz* ratings influence dispute costs.

Conclusion

The past 15 years have seen much change and upheaval in the California workers' compensation system, particularly the compensation of permanent partial disability benefits. Competing concerns about benefit adequacy and employer cost have motivated numerous reform efforts. At times, these reforms have addressed one issue while worsening the other. This report evaluated how the changes to disability benefits in S.B. 863 will effect outcomes for injured workers, and found that they largely offset the declines in benefit adequacy that occurred in the wake of S.B. 899. However, remaining issues with the California system need to be addressed in order to ensure that disabled workers receive adequate and fair compensation that is administered in an efficient fashion and that is affordable to employers and the public.

Methods and Supplemental Results for Chapter Three

Construction of Matched Wage Data

The DWC created files containing identifiers for individuals appearing in the WCIS or the DEU and securely transferred these files to the State of California EDD for linkage to wage histories for injured workers and matched controls. All steps involving identifiable information (name and SSN) took place at EDD; names were removed and Social Security numbers were scrambled before any files were transferred to RAND.

The starting point for constructing the WCIS analysis file is the WCIS injured worker file, containing identifying information (name and Social Security number) and injury dates for approximately 9 million selected workers injured between 2005 and 2014, and the quarterly wage history data covering all workers from 1995 through 2014. Starting with the WCIS injured worker file, we applied several screening steps to eliminate bad or malformed SSNs and eliminate exact duplicates based on SSN and year-of-injury. This reduced the file by less than 1 percent. Next, we limited the population to those workers injured from 2005 through 2013—yielding approximately 4.3 million workers.

We then pulled quarterly wages for these workers from the EDD wage history files covering the entire 1995–2014 period. The wage files are very large and these wage pulls took a considerable amount of time. Wages were pulled by merging to the EDD wage data using SSN, dropping workers who matched to no wage records in any quarter. This step also created two-character Soundex strings based on a worker's first and last name in each wage quarter. These Soundex strings were used to ensure the integrity of the wage data by checking for consistency of worker names across the quarterly wage records. Workers with inconsistent names across their wage histories were dropped later in the file-building process.

The resulting merged wage history file for workers injured between 2005 and 2013 was downloaded to RAND using a secure, encrypted Accellion server. The IDs on the file at this point for each worker were a jurisdiction claim number (JCN) and a scrambled SSN named SSN_KEY. The unscrambled SSN remained at EDD.

When downloaded, the WCIS file structure consisted of quarterly wage records, with each worker represented by up to 80 quarters of wage data. The next step was to construct a JCN-level file with one record per JCN and 80 quarters of wage history data strung out on each record. This wide file was then merged to the data from FROI and SROI provided by DWC. The FROI and SROI files were merged using JCN.

As mentioned above, earlier in the file-building process, we constructed Soundex string based on worker first and last names. Actual first and last names were not included on the file downloaded to RAND for confidentiality reasons: only the Soundex strings were transferred. At this point, we built indicators based on the consistency of the two-character Soundex strings of first and last names across the EDD wage history data for a given worker. The process cycled through the quarterly wage history data and set various flags to identify inconstancies observed in worker first and last names. The flags were used during the analysis phase of the project to screen out workers with inconsistencies in their names. In order to qualify for inclusion, only those workers were included whose history included either a single, consistent last name across the entire wage history, or multiple last names but a single consistent first name (allowing for the possibility of last name changes due to marriage).

We allowed first name–last name flip-flops (e.g., "Adam Smith" and "Smith Adam" were treated as the same worker), and we treated single initials as equivalent to the same first name (e.g., "Adam Smith" and "A. Smith" were considered the same worker).

Name consistency was not checked for the entire eighty-quarter wage history. Instead, we looked at different windows of wage quarters. Wider windows, with more wage quarters, would be more likely to yield name inconsistencies, while narrower windows would be more generous. After experimenting with several different window sizes, we selected the period plus/minus eight wage quarters surrounding the quarter of injury. Workers with inconsistent names within this wage window were not included in the analysis.

Control Worker Selection and Match Quality

As described in Chapter Three, our procedure for estimating earnings losses due to injury involves selecting a control group of workers who did not experience a workplace injury. This appendix provides additional details on the procedure used to select matched controls and presents some measures of match quality.

For each injured worker with a match to the EDD base wage file, our matching algorithm consists of the following steps:

1. select the earnings histories of all workers with earnings from the at-injury employer in the quarter of injury
2. for each *potential control* worker selected in step 1, calculate total earnings from all employers over the four quarters immediately preceding the quarter of injury. We refer to this time period as the *match window*.
3. for each potential control worker selected in step 1, calculate the difference between the natural log of total earnings over the match window and the natural log of the injured worker's total earnings over the match window
4. exclude any potential control workers for whom the difference calculated in step 3 is greater than 20 percent of the standard deviation of the log of injured worker yearly earnings over the match window
5. for each potential control worker remaining after step 4, calculate pre-injury tenure at the at-injury employer as the number of consecutive quarters of earnings at the at-injury employer
6. exclude any potential control workers for whom pre-injury tenure differs from the injured worker, with tenure coded into three categories (less than or equal to one year on the job, one to two years, or more than two years)
7. for each potential control worker remaining after step 6, rank control workers by their distance from the injured worker's profile of quarterly earnings over each quarter in the match window
8. select the five closest matches according to the ranking in step 7 and discard the remaining control workers.

We apply steps 1 through 8 for each injured worker matched to a valid wage history, sampling control workers with replacement. In order to summarize in a single number the distance between the paths of injured and control worker earnings over the match window, we use the Mahalanobis distance in step 7. The Mahalanobis distance, which is widely used in the literature on matching when the match is based on more than one variable, can be thought of as a generalization of the Euclidean distance that corrects for the variance and covariance of each element of the vector used for matching.[1] To understand how this distance measure is constructed and how it ranks the potential control workers, define vectors $\vec{y}^I$ and $\vec{y}^U$ containing total earnings in each of the four quarters preceding the quarter of injury t_0 for each potential control worker ($\vec{y}^U$) and the corresponding injured worker ($\vec{y}^I$)

$$\vec{y}^U = (y^U_{(t_0-1)}, y^U_{(t_0-2)}, y^U_{(t_0-3)}, y^U_{(t_0-4)})'$$
$$\vec{y}^I = (y^I_{(t_0-1)}, y^I_{(t_0-2)}, y^I_{(t_0-3)}, y^I_{(t_0-4)})'$$

The Mahalanobis distance M between each potential control and the injured worker is then defined by

$$M = (\vec{y}^I - \vec{y}^U)' \hat{\Sigma}_y^{-1} (\vec{y}^I - \vec{y}^U)$$

where $\hat{\Sigma}_y$ denotes the sample covariance matrix of $\vec{y}^I$ for injured workers with the same quarter of injury. The Mahalanobis distance is a slight departure from the distance measures applied in previous RAND reports that used the matching methodology, which used the average wage over the match window as the basis for ranking. The difference is that the Mahalanobis distance incorporates information about the quarter-by-quarter distance between potential control worker earnings and injured worker earnings, thus prioritizing potential controls who experience similar earnings growth to the injured worker in addition to selecting workers with similar annual earnings.

Match quality can be evaluated using statistics that summarize the distance between the injured and control workers. We examine three such statistics: average imbalance after matching, average absolute imbalance after matching, and average elementwise absolute imbalance after matching. The average imbalance after matching is the average difference between injured and control worker annual earnings. A more stringent criterion is the average absolute imbalance, which uses the absolute value of the difference in annual earnings instead. Finally, we also present the elementwise absolute imbalance, which sums the absolute value of the difference in quarterly earnings between injured and control. Formally, these are defined as follows:

$$\text{Average Imbalance} = \frac{1}{N} \sum_{i=1}^{N} (1,1,1,1)(\vec{y}^I - \vec{y}^U)$$

$$\text{Average Absolute Imbalance} = \frac{1}{N} \sum_{i=1}^{N} \left| (1,1,1,1)(\vec{y}^I - \vec{y}^U) \right|$$

$$\text{Average Elementwise Absolute Imbalance} = \frac{1}{N} \sum_{i=1}^{N} \sum_{\tau=1}^{4} \left| y^I_{t_0-\tau} - y^U_{t_0-\tau} \right|$$

----

[1] See Lee (2005), pp. 85–87.

Table A.1 presents match quality statistics for the WCIS and DEU samples. The top panel presents imbalance statistics calculated over the match window, while the lower panel presents imbalance statistics calculated over the year preceding the match window. The imbalance statistics for the match window verify our success in finding close matches for injured workers; the statistics for the year preceding the match window address the plausibility of the matching assumption that workers with similar wage profiles during the match window have similar earnings at other points in time. Imbalance statistics are reported as percentages of average earnings for all injured workers in the relevant sample over the time period for which the imbalance statistics are calculated.

Table A.1 shows that the quality of the match for both samples is high. The average imbalance in the match window is below 1 percent in both the WCIS sample (0.6 percent of injured worker earnings) and the DEU sample (0.1 percent of injured worker earnings). The average absolute imbalance over the match window, which captures the average distance between injured and control workers at the individual level (in contrast to the group-level comparison captured in the average imbalance) is also quite low. The average matched worker in the WCIS has controls whose annual earnings were within 4.1 percent (roughly $1,700) of average injured worker earnings over the match window; the corresponding figure for the DEU is 2.8 percent (roughly $1,300). The elementwise absolute imbalance, which captures the average distance on an individual, quarter-by-quarter basis, is somewhat higher, at 10.3 percent of average earnings in the WCIS and 8.9 percent in the DEU.

The lower panel of Table A.1 shows that the average imbalance was also quite low over the year preceding the match window: the difference in average annual earnings for both the WCIS and DEU samples remains below 1 percent of average injured worker earnings. Because

Table A.1
Match Quality for WCIS and DEU Matched Controls

	WCIS	DEU
Balance Statistics for Match Window (1–4 Quarters Pre-Injury)		
Average Imbalance (%)	0.6	0.1
Average Absolute Imbalance (%)	4.1	2.8
Average Elementwise Absolute Imbalance (%)	10.3	8.9
Balance Statistics for Year Before Match Window (5–8 Quarters Pre-Injury)		
Average Imbalance (%)	0.8	0.8
Average Absolute Imbalance (%)	20.9	17.6
Average Elementwise Absolute Imbalance (%)	25.7	21.8

NOTES: All average balance statistics reported as percentages of average annual earnings for injured workers over the same time period. Balance defined as difference between injured and control worker annual earnings. Absolute balance defined as absolute difference between injured and control worker annual earnings. Elementwise absolute balance defined as sum of absolute value of difference between injured and control worker quarterly earnings over one year. Match window contains earnings records 1 to 4 quarters prior to the quarter of injury. Year before match window contains earnings records 5 to 8 quarters prior to the quarter of injury.

we did not use any data on the level of wages from this time period to choose the matched controls, we view this as a validation of our matching methodology. That said, the absolute imbalance and elementwise absolute imbalance are several times larger over the year preceding the match period.

The average imbalance is the least demanding matching criterion we consider in that positive and negative differences for different workers can cancel each other out. However, for our purposes, the average imbalance is arguably the most relevant measure, since all our estimates average many injured workers together (thus allowing poor matches at the individual level to cancel out). We included the average absolute imbalance and the average elementwise imbalance so that technical readers can understand the quality of the match at the individual level.

As an alternative approach to evaluating the plausibility of the matching method used here, we can conduct a "placebo" exercise in which we compare one control worker's earnings to average earnings for the remaining matched controls. Although we cannot test the assumption that injured and control worker earnings would have followed the same trajectory in the absence of an injury, we can examine whether the control workers' earnings continue to move together after the injury. To do so, we recalculated control worker wages excluding each injured worker's best match (under the algorithm described above) from the control set and then calculated the difference between the best control's earnings and the other controls. Results for the average difference over the two years before and two years after the injury are presented in Table A.2. Average earnings evolve similarly after the date of injury for the best control and the remaining controls, providing additional support for the plausibility of our match assumption.

Long-Term Earnings Loss Trajectories

To evaluate the potential for bias due to our focus on a short follow-up period, we examined long-term earnings profiles for workers injured in 2008 or earlier, for whom we obtained five or more years of post-injury data. These data, presented in Figures A.1–A.3, show that injured and control worker earnings profiles are very close to parallel after the second post-injury year. For earnings and employment, relative outcomes in the second post-injury year may be a reasonable proxy for long-term relative outcomes. Relative at-injury employment continues to decline steadily through the fifth post-injury year.

Methodology for Case-Mix Adjustment of Time Profile of Relative Earnings

To assess the effect of covariates on injured worker outcomes, our primary regression specification for the effect of injury on labor market outcomes uses the difference between injured and control worker outcomes as the dependent variable.

$$y_{ijqt}^I - y_{ijqt}^C = f(E^{I,\text{pre-injury}}, \beta^E) + X_i^D \beta^D + X_i^I \beta^I + X_{jq}^F \beta^F + \mu_q + \varepsilon_{ijqt}$$

where

y_{ijqt}^I Injured worker outcome yt quarters post-injury for injured worker i injured at firm j in quarter q

y_{ijqt}^C Control worker outcome yt quarters post-injury for injured worker i injured at firm j in quarter q

$f(E^{I,\text{pre-injury}}, \beta^E)$ Flexible function for injured worker's real pre-injury annual earnings (dummy variables for 50 bins)

X_i^D Dummy variables for demographics of injured worker, including gender and five-year age bins

X_i^I Controls for characteristics of injury, including receipt of TTD benefits, estimated TTD duration (dummy variables for ten deciles of implied TTD duration), number of permanent impairments reported in WCIS (zero, one, or two), and dummy variables for body part of injury (55 categories)

X_{jq}^F Controls for characteristics of at-injury firm in the quarter of injury, including dummies for seven bins of firm size, ten industry categories, seven bins of the firm's cumulative growth rate over the year preceding the injury, and four bins of the firm's quarterly separation rate over the year preceding the injury.[2]

In models for earnings loss, y denotes total annual earnings over the first, second, or third full post-injury year. In models for employment (at-injury employment), y^I denotes a dummy variable for the event that the injured worker is working (employed at the at-injury firm) in the fourth, eighth, or twelfth post-injury quarter. y^C is the fraction of the injured worker's matched control workers who are working (employed at the at-injury firm) in the same quarter.

Construction of Temporary Disability Duration and Additional Summary Statistics on Injury Characteristics

We provide some additional detail and summary statistics on the procedures we used to construct selected covariates for use in our regression models for earnings loss.

To control for changes in the initial severity of injury, we calculated the duration of temporary total disability implied by the WCIS data. TTD duration variables used in this study are meant as a proxy for the initial severity of the disability to be used in the absence of reliable PD rating information about the case. We used data on the total amounts of TTD benefits paid to date (including settlements) and data reported in the WCIS on the average weekly wage to calculate the implied duration of temporary total disability (applying the SAWW-indexed weekly minimum and maximum corresponding to each year of injury as appropriate).

---

[2]   All dummy variable sets exclude one category.

Table B.1
Definition of Implied TTD Duration Control Variables and Average Durations and Paid-to-Date Amounts by Decile of Implied Duration

TTD Duration Category	Minimum Implied Duration	Maximum Implied Duration*	Average Implied Weeks* TTD	TTD Paid-to-Date (BTC 050)	TTD Settlement Paid-to-Date (BTC 550)	Percentage of PPD Cases (Weighted)
No TTD payments	0.0	0.0	0.0	0.0	0.0	29.2
1	0.0	3.0	1.3	637.1	14.2	7.1
2	3.0	7.5	5.1	2416.0	65.8	7.0
3	7.5	12.7	10.0	4589.7	106.9	7.0
4	12.7	19.2	15.8	7170.1	148.1	7.0
5	19.2	27.6	23.2	10159.1	225.1	7.0
6	27.6	38.4	32.7	14020.7	287.3	7.1
7	38.4	52.1	45.1	18905.1	448.3	7.1
8	52.1	72.5	61.5	25247.9	456.2	7.1
9	72.5	103.9	87.8	36026.3	473.9	7.2
10	103.9	104.0	104.0	396248.4	811.9	7.3

* Winsorized at 104 weeks.

This process is potentially prone to measurement error deriving both from the paid amounts and from the weekly wage variable. On claims with injury dates toward the end of the sample, a mild amount of right-truncation is also likely for the most serious cases. To reduce the effect of these forms of measurement error and truncation, we binned the implied TTD duration into deciles for use as a case-mix-adjustment variable. Because TTD durations are so right-skewed, the effect of right-censoring on injury durations in 2011 and 2012 is likely to be confined to the top two or three deciles of the TTD duration distribution. We enter these implied TTD duration deciles into our regression model as a set of dummy variables, with the excluded category being PPD cases with no paid TTD at the time of data collection. Table B.1 reports boundaries for the categories of implied TTD duration used as control variables. The average paid to date amounts for the top decile are implausibly high, reflecting some extremely large outlier amounts. Because we work with binned values of implied duration, these outliers should not affect our results as long as these cases are generally high-severity.

To examine whether right-truncation drives trends in implied TTD duration, we compared trends in the average TTD duration to trends at lower percentiles. Right-truncation in later injury years should lead to underestimates of total paid amounts (and therefore of implied TTD duration) primarily for cases that are still being paid at the time of truncation. Some lower-duration cases could also be affected because TTD for an injury may occur after an initial attempt at return to work, but we are comfortable assuming that right-truncation would appear as a differential decrease in cases with implied durations high enough to extend beyond 104 weeks after the date of injury.

Table B.2 shows average implied duration and selected percentiles of duration by year of injury among permanently disabled workers who receive TTD benefits. The decline in average TTD duration that initially raised our concerns about right-truncation is apparent among cases with low and high implied duration alike and begins in 2010. The decline in the average duration closely mirrors the decline in the median, and changes between 2009 and 2012 at the

Table B.2
Implied TTD Duration by Year of Injury

Injury Year	Average	10th Percentile	25th Percentile	Median	75th Percentile
2005	37.7	3.1	10.1	27.1	58.3
2006	38.2	3.0	10.0	27.0	60.3
2007	39.1	2.9	10.0	28.0	62.6
2008	41.6	3.1	10.7	30.5	68.9
2009	41.2	3.3	10.7	30.3	67.3
2010	39.9	2.9	10.0	28.8	64.0
2011	38.7	2.8	9.8	27.6	61.3
2012	33.4	2.5	8.3	23.4	50.7

NOTE: Implied TTD duration winsorized at 104 weeks.

25th percentile are similar to those observed at the median in percentage terms. Table B.2 suggests that a general decline in implied TTD duration drives the trend in the average, not right-truncation.

We emphasize that the figures reported in Tables B.1 and B.2 are to be used as a rough proxy for initial injury severity. Inferring the actual duration of total disability from administrative data on paid amounts is an inherently error-prone process, and we caution against treating these data directly as a measure of time spent on TTD for the average worker. It is also worth repeating that these are estimates for the population of workers who also receive PPD indemnity payments or settled PPD payments, and not for the overall population of workers with TTD indemnity payments. These cases are much higher-severity on average, and it is not at all clear that average TTD duration for PPD cases should move together with overall average TTD duration.

We also report the incidence of part of injury codes by period (pre-recession, recession, post-recession) in Table B.3. Body part of injury is reported on the FROI, and so it is a rough proxy for the type of permanent impairment. The relative frequencies of the most common body parts of injury among the PPD population are fairly stable across period, though some injury types (soft tissue neck injuries, shoulder injuries, lower back injuries, and knee injuries) do become slightly more common after the recession. This table is included primarily as a benchmarking resource for other analysts interested in California's workers' compensation system.

Injured workers with missing data on any of the included covariates were dropped from the sample. This resulted in the exclusion of 17,672 observations, or 5.4 percent of the 345,282 injuries used to calculate the overall time profile of relative earnings in Chapter Four. The fraction of otherwise eligible observations dropped is highest in 2005 (8 percent) and 2006 (6 percent) but then stabilizes between 3 and 5 percent for each year from 2007 to 2012. Pre-recession relative earnings for the regression sample are slightly lower (72.7 percent) than for the sample used to estimate the overall time profile of relative earnings (73.7 percent), but match the overall averages very closely in later years.

The higher rate of missing industry codes in earlier years raises the possibility of survivorship bias in the selection of firms for our regression analysis sample: EDD retains industry codes for only five years, so we had to backfill NAICS codes to employers in earlier years. Missing NAICS codes may be differentially likely for firms that went out of business or changed tax ID number between the date of injury and 2009, which was the earliest quarter with NAICS

Table B.3
Injury Part of Body Codes by Period

	Pre-Recession (2005–2007) (%)	Recession (2008–2009) (%)	Post-Recession (2010–2012) (%)	Total (%)
25: Soft tissue neck	1.1	1.4	1.6	1.3
30: Multiple upper extremities	3.1	2.8	2.7	2.9
31: Upper arm	1.5	1.5	1.5	1.5
32: Elbow	1.9	1.8	1.8	1.8
33: Lower arm	2.0	1.9	2.0	2.0
34: Wrist	4.7	4.8	4.6	4.7
35: Hand	3.8	3.5	3.6	3.6
36: Finger(s)	4.0	3.9	4.0	4.0
37: Thumb	1.2	1.2	1.1	1.2
38: Shoulder(s)	9.6	10.5	11.0	10.3
39: Wrist(s) & hand(s)	1.5	1.5	1.4	1.5
41: Upper back area	3.0	2.1	1.8	2.4
42: Lower back area	15.3	16.1	16.7	16.0
53: Knee	11.6	12.1	12.5	12.0
54: Lower leg	1.4	1.3	1.3	1.3
55: Ankle	2.7	2.7	2.6	2.7
56: Foot	2.0	1.9	1.8	1.9
66: No physical injury	0.9	1.2	1.4	1.2
90: Multiple body parts	13.8	13.1	12.5	13.2
Other*	14.9	14.6	14.1	14.6

* All "other" part of injury codes each represent less than 1% of injuries.

codes in the EDD data.[3] Examining post-injury outcomes for the control workers at firms with missing NAICS codes confirms that these firms had differentially poor outcomes for control workers, as one might expect if these firms were more likely to go out of business. In this case, survivorship bias in the sample of employers used for our regression models leads us to exclude workers with relatively *small* earnings losses in the early years of the sample. This would lead us to *underestimate* relative earnings (i.e., overestimate earnings losses) for injured workers in the early years with more missing NAICS codes, since the injured workers who are excluded from the sample would have experienced earnings losses in the absence of their injuries when their employers went out of business. We reiterate that this problem does not affect our main estimates of unadjusted trends (since we do not require complete data on covariates for those estimates), nor does it affect any of the estimates in Chapters Three, Five, or Six.

This potential bias is not a problem for the internal validity of our case-mix-adjustment model, our regression estimates, or our decomposition results quantifying the contribution of compositional changes to the time profile of earnings losses. Assuming that non-reporting of

---

[3]   The FROI contains an industry code field as well. Unfortunately, industry reporting on the FROI is missing for 59 percent of 2005 injuries and 40 percent of 2006 injuries that would otherwise be usable in our regression sample, and so we do not use it in our analysis.

NAICS codes to EDD for reasons other than attrition of firms is random, then our case-mix-adjustment and decomposition results are valid for the population of workers injured at employers that survived to 2009. This population covers the vast majority of injured workers. In 2005, the year with the highest share of missing NAICS data, the share of missing cases is 8.2 percent, 5 percentage points higher than the 3.2-percent rate for injuries in 2009 or later (when there is no survivorship bias).

The main consequence of survivorship bias due to non-reporting of NAICS codes is that our decomposition results may not be externally valid for the full population of PPD cases. Intuition suggests that survivorship bias would lead us to slightly overestimate the role of compositional factors because the unadjusted drop in relative earnings associated with the Great Recession is in fact larger than the unadjusted drop observed in our regression sample. However, this line of reasoning is not conclusive without knowledge of whether the employers that are excluded from the sample because they went out of business are in industries with relatively high or relatively low earnings losses.

However, because the missing data problem affects relatively few cases, the effect is likely to be very small. To illustrate the potential effect of this bias on our decomposition results, we added the difference in pre-recession earnings losses to the total change between pre- and post-recession outcomes estimated in the regression sample (and used to calculate the decomposition results in Table 4.6). Under the assumption that this difference in unadjusted wage loss between the regression sample and the full PPD sample is uncorrelated with all explanatory variables (i.e., it is purely the effect of changing economic conditions), we can recalculate the decomposition results in Table 4.6 to obtain an (approximate) lower bound on the change in average earnings losses from the pre- to post-recession that is explained by compositional factors.[4] This back-of-the-envelope calculation implies that at least 40 percent of the change in average earnings losses for permanently disabled workers can be attributed to compositional factors, in contrast to the 46-percent estimate for the regression sample that is reported in Table 4.6. Since this difference is fairly small compared to the range of estimates already reported using alternative outcome definitions (in Table B.4, dropping the recession years from the sample), we do not believe that survivorship bias affects the qualitative conclusions that we draw from our decomposition results.

Regression Estimates for Association Between Worker Characteristics and Post-Injury Outcomes

Table B.4 shows parameter estimates for the coefficients on age and gender. Because we are not explicitly matching on age and gender, these estimates should not be interpreted as the causal effects of age or gender on earnings losses, but rather as potentially contaminated by omitted variable bias. For instance, if older workers nearing retirement age matched to younger workers with longer remaining careers, the effect of age on earnings loss would be biased downward. However, these coefficients do capture all the variation in outcomes that is predicted by demographics, and therefore can be used for case-mix adjustment.

Table B.5 shows the effects on earnings loss of proxies for injury severity and type of injury that are observable in the WCIS: temporary disability duration, number of permanent impairments reported on the SROI, and body part of injury reported on the FROI.

---

[4]   The average difference between pre- and post-recession earnings loss in the regression sample is 6.3 percentage points, and the change predicted by the change in average covariates is 2.9 percentage points. The estimate in Table 4.6 is 2.9/6.3 = 46 percent. If we add 1.0 percentage points to the pre-recession loss and perform this calculation, we obtain 2.9/7.3 = 40 percent.

Table B.4
Regression Coefficients for Demographics (Age at Injury and Gender) and Job Tenure

Variables	Annual Earnings: Difference from Control Workers			Employment: Difference from Control Workers			At-Injury Employment: Difference from Control Workers		
	First Post-Injury Year	Second Post-Injury Year	Third Post-Injury Year	Fourth Post-Injury Quarter	Eighth Post-Injury Quarter	Twelfth Post-Injury Quarter	Fourth Post-Injury Quarter	Eighth Post-Injury Quarter	Twelfth Post-Injury Quarter
Female	960.9***	–373.2***	–457.7***	0.00974***	–0.00158	–0.00577**	0.0144***	0.00867***	0.00305
	–91.56	–111.8	–129.1	–0.00204	–0.00217	–0.00236	–0.00206	–0.00209	–0.00214
	[781.4–1,140]	[–592.3––154.0]	[–710.7––204.6]	[0.00575–0.0137]	[–0.00584–0.00268]	[–0.0104––0.00115]	[0.0104–0.0185]	[0.00458–0.0128]	[–0.00114–0.00725]
Age excluded group: Ages 16–20									
Age 21–25	512.8*	804.9**	1,091**	–0.0342***	–0.0506***	–0.0324***	0.011	0.00502	0.00673
	–296.3	–350.7	–427.6	–0.0102	–0.0109	–0.0115	–0.0101	–0.00936	–0.00904
	[–67.95–1,094]	[117.6–1,492]	[252.5–1,929]	[–0.0543––0.0142]	[–0.0720––0.0292]	[–0.0549––0.00990]	[–0.00873–0.0308]	[–0.0133–0.0234]	[–0.0110–0.0245]
Age 26–30	1,123***	1,356***	1,500***	–0.0564***	–0.0816***	–0.0668***	0.014	0.0168*	0.0220**
	–288.4	–341	–424.3	–0.00988	–0.0105	–0.0111	–0.00972	–0.00904	–0.00871
	[557.9–1,688]	[687.8–2,024]	[668.3–2,332]	[–0.0757––0.0370]	[–0.102––0.0610]	[–0.0886––0.0451]	[–0.00504–0.0331]	[–0.000920–0.0345]	[0.00497–0.0391]
Age 31–35	1,105***	1,377***	1,312***	–0.0589***	–0.0951***	–0.0797***	0.0233**	0.0285***	0.0349***
	–288.3	–339	–416.8	–0.00976	–0.0104	–0.011	–0.0096	–0.00894	–0.00861
	[540.1–1,670]	[712.5–2,041]	[495.0–2,129]	[–0.0781––0.0398]	[–0.116––0.0747]	[–0.101––0.0583]	[0.00445–0.0421]	[0.0109–0.0460]	[0.0180–0.0517]
Age 36–40	1,033***	1,536***	1,492***	–0.0613***	–0.0961***	–0.0824***	0.0244***	0.0399***	0.0468***
	–281.8	–332.3	–411.6	–0.00966	–0.0103	–0.0108	–0.0095	–0.00884	–0.00851
	[480.7–1,585]	[884.7–2,187]	[685.6–2,299]	[–0.0802––0.0424]	[–0.116––0.0759]	[–0.104––0.0612]	[0.00575–0.0430]	[0.0226–0.0572]	[0.0301–0.0634]

Table B.4—Continued

Variables	Annual Earnings: Difference from Control Workers			Employment: Difference from Control Workers			At-Injury Employment: Difference from Control Workers		
	First Post-Injury Year	Second Post-Injury Year	Third Post-Injury Year	Fourth Post-Injury Quarter	Eighth Post-Injury Quarter	Twelfth Post-Injury Quarter	Fourth Post-Injury Quarter	Eighth Post-Injury Quarter	Twelfth Post-Injury Quarter
Age 41–45	1,084***	1,373***	960.7**	−0.0602***	−0.103***	−0.0990***	0.0323***	0.0437***	0.0478***
	−278.3	−328.6	−406.4	−0.00959	−0.0102	−0.0108	−0.00943	−0.00877	−0.00844
	[533.2–1,629]	[729.1–2,017]	[164.2–1,757]	[−0.0790−−0.0414]	[−0.123−−0.0831]	[−0.120−−0.0779]	[0.0138–0.0507]	[0.0265–0.0609]	[0.0312–0.0643]
Age 46–50	1,153***	678.6**	−765.7*	−0.0601***	−0.118***	−0.125***	0.0414***	0.0492***	0.0517***
	−278.4	−327.9	−407	−0.00957	−0.0102	−0.0107	−0.00941	−0.00875	−0.00843
	[607.7–1,699]	[35.98–1,321]	[−1,563–32.12]	[−0.0788−−0.0413]	[−0.138−−0.0977]	[−0.146−−0.104]	[0.0229–0.0598]	[0.0321–0.0664]	[0.0352–0.0682]
Age 51–55	567.7**	−1,669***	−4,764***	−0.0706***	−0.150***	−0.179***	0.0341***	0.0275***	0.0153*
	−281	−332.6	−412.4	−0.00959	−0.0102	−0.0108	−0.00943	−0.00879	−0.00847
	[16.90–1,119]	[−2,321−−1,017]	[−5,572−−3,956]	[−0.0894−−0.0518]	[−0.170−−0.130]	[−0.200−−0.158]	[0.0156−0.0526]	[0.0103−0.0448]	[−0.00133−0.0319]
Age 56–60	−260.5	−4,386***	−8,543***	−0.0941***	−0.197***	−0.247***	0.0179*	0.000713	−0.0183**
	−250.4	−345.2	−426.1	−0.0097	−0.0104	−0.0109	−0.00955	−0.00892	−0.00863
	[−829.7–308.6]	[−5,063−−3,709]	[−9,378−−7,707]	[−0.113−−0.0751]	[−0.217−−0.177]	[−0.268−−0.225]	[−0.000851−0.0366]	[−0.0168−0.0182]	[−0.0352−−0.00137]
Age 61–65	−2,005***	−8,041***	−12,907***	−0.134***	−0.275***	−0.343***	−0.0138	−0.0561***	−0.0859***
	−323.8	−388.7	−466.3	−0.0101	−0.0108	−0.0114	−0.00998	−0.00944	−0.00919
	[−2,640−−1,371]	[−8,803−−7,279]	[−13,821−−11,993]	[−0.154−−0.114]	[−0.296−−0.254]	[−0.365−−0.321]	[−0.0334−0.00571]	[−0.0746−−0.0376]	[−0.104−−0.0678]
Age 66–70	−2,473***	−7,838***	−12,567***	−0.145***	−0.282***	−0.349***	−0.0234**	−0.0618***	−0.0863***
	−422.4	−507	−601.1	−0.012	−0.0127	−0.0134	−0.0119	−0.0116	−0.0115
	[−3,301−−1,645]	[−8,832−−6,844]	[−13,745−−11,389]	[−0.168−−0.122]	[−0.307−−0.257]	[−0.375−−0.323]	[−0.0467−−2.09e−05]	[−0.0845−−0.0391]	[−0.109−−0.0639]

Table B.4—Continued

Variables	Annual Earnings: Difference from Control Workers			Employment: Difference from Control Workers			At-Injury Employment: Difference from Control Workers		
	First Post-Injury Year	Second Post-Injury Year	Third Post-Injury Year	Fourth Post-Injury Quarter	Eighth Post-Injury Quarter	Twelfth Post-Injury Quarter	Fourth Post-Injury Quarter	Eighth Post-Injury Quarter	Twelfth Post-Injury Quarter
Pre-Injury Job Tenure excluded group: 1–2Q									
Pre-injury job tenure 2–3Q	−404.9**	−658.1***	−582.5**	−0.00940**	−0.0145***	−0.0201***	0.0196***	0.0137***	0.00432
	(185.7)	(218.9)	(242.2)	(0.00476)	(0.00495)	(0.00523)	(0.00471)	(0.00436)	(0.00420)
	[−769.0 – −40.87]	[−1,087 – −229.0]	[−1,057 – −107.8]	[−0.0187 – −7.21e−05]	[−0.0242 – −0.00478]	[−0.0304 – −0.00987]	[0.0103 – 0.0288]	[0.00520 – 0.0223]	[−0.00391 – 0.0126]
Pre-injury job tenure 4–5Q	2,017***	1,495***	1,280***	−0.0626***	−0.0767***	−0.0803***	−0.0859***	−0.106***	−0.112***
	(204.6)	(244.7)	(273.5)	(0.00506)	(0.00536)	(0.00569)	(0.00509)	(0.00490)	(0.00482)
	[1,617 – 2,418]	[1,015 – 1,974]	[743.7 – 1,816]	[−0.0725 – −0.0527]	[−0.0872 – −0.0662]	[−0.0914 – −0.0691]	[−0.0958 – −0.0759]	[−0.115 – −0.0959]	[−0.121 – −0.103]
Pre-injury job tenure 6–7Q	1,394***	1,199***	1,250***	−0.0611***	−0.0783***	−0.0811***	−0.0849***	−0.107***	−0.119***
	(220.1)	(261.5)	(294.4)	(0.00537)	(0.00565)	(0.00600)	(0.00542)	(0.00521)	(0.00516)
	[963.0 – 1,826]	[686.2 – 1,711]	[672.7 – 1,827]	[−0.0717 – −0.0506]	[−0.0894 – −0.0673]	[−0.0929 – −0.0693]	[−0.0956 – −0.0743]	[−0.118 – −0.0972]	[−0.129 – −0.109]
Pre-injury job tenure 8Q+	3,424***	3,221***	2,969***	−0.0263***	−0.0481***	−0.0575***	−0.0294***	−0.0453***	−0.0584***
	(181.3)	(214.4)	(237.4)	(0.00422)	(0.00444)	(0.00468)	(0.00424)	(0.00405)	(0.00397)
	[3,069 – 3,780]	[2,801 – 3,642]	[2,504 – 3,434]	[−0.0346 – −0.0181]	[−0.0568 – −0.0394]	[−0.0667 – −0.0483]	[−0.0377 – −0.0211]	[−0.0532 – −0.0374]	[−0.0662 – −0.0507]
Observations	327,520	327,521	304,177	327,520	327,554	304,210	327,520	327,554	304,210
R-squared	0.182	0.13	0.107	0.152	0.122	0.098	0.117	0.098	0.087

NOTES: Robust standard errors in parentheses. 95% confidence intervals in brackets. Outcome variables in regressions are differences between injured worker and control worker outcomes at selected post-injury time horizons; positive coefficients mean that higher values of the explanatory variables predict better outcomes for injured workers relative to controls. Regression models do not include time effects. Regression specifications are otherwise identical to those used for Tables B.5–B.7. Control variables not reported include pre-injury annual earnings (50 categories), gender, age, at-injury firm size, at-injury firm growth rate, at-injury firm separation rate, industry fixed effects, deciles of temporary disability duration, number of permanent impairments, and body part of injury.

*** $p < 0.01$, ** $p < 0.05$, * $p < 0.1$

Table B.5
Regression Coefficients for Injury Characteristics

Variables	Annual Earnings: Difference from Control Workers			Employment: Difference from Control Workers			At-Injury Employment: Difference from Control Workers		
	First Post-Injury Year	Second Post-Injury Year	Third Post-Injury Year	Fourth Post-Injury Quarter	Eighth Post-Injury Quarter	Twelfth Post-Injury Quarter	Fourth Post-Injury Quarter	Eighth Post-Injury Quarter	Twelfth Post-Injury Quarter
Decile of total disability duration excluded group: No paid TTD									
TTD Duration Decile 1	283.2	232.0	−2.165	0.0533***	0.0426***	0.0339***	0.0583***	0.0506***	0.0387***
	(185.0)	(229.4)	(263.6)	(0.00376)	(0.00417)	(0.00458)	(0.00392)	(0.00412)	(0.00432)
	[−79.39–645.7]	[−217.5–681.5]	[−518.9–514.6]	[0.0460–0.0607]	[0.0344–0.0507]	[0.0249–0.0429]	[0.0506–0.0660]	[0.0426–0.0587]	[0.0303–0.0472]
TTD Duration Decile 2	−677.1***	−272.9	−456.3*	0.0465***	0.0423***	0.0339***	0.0583***	0.0535***	0.0424***
	(174.7)	(216.9)	(253.3)	(0.00377)	(0.00412)	(0.00451)	(0.00393)	(0.00410)	(0.00431)
	[−1,019––334.8]	[−698.0–152.3]	[−952.9–40.22]	[0.0392–0.0539]	[0.0342–0.0504]	[0.0250–0.0427]	[0.0506–0.0660]	[0.0455–0.0615]	[0.0339–0.0508]
TTD Duration Decile 3	−2,581***	−1,132***	−1,516***	0.0379***	0.0274***	0.0176***	0.0574***	0.0445***	0.0318***
	(168.2)	(210.9)	(246.9)	(0.00378)	(0.00416)	(0.00451)	(0.00391)	(0.00411)	(0.00430)
	[−2,910––2,251]	[−1,545––718.4]	[−2,000––1,032]	[0.0305–0.0453]	[0.0193–0.0356]	[0.00877–0.0265]	[0.0498–0.0651]	[0.0364–0.0525]	[0.0233–0.0402]
TTD Duration Decile 4	−5,301***	−2,679***	−2,703***	0.0198***	0.0113***	0.00278	0.0380***	0.0278***	0.0107**
	(169.8)	(211.5)	(246.6)	(0.00393)	(0.00421)	(0.00459)	(0.00401)	(0.00412)	(0.00430)
	[−5,633––4,968]	[−3,094––2,265]	[−3,186––2,220]	[0.0121–0.0275]	[0.00308–0.0196]	[−0.00620–0.0118]	[0.0301–0.0458]	[0.0197–0.0359]	[0.00226–0.0191]
TTD Duration Decile 5	−9,003***	−5,505***	−4,714***	−0.0429***	−0.0388***	−0.0361***	−0.0113***	−0.0221***	−0.0256***
	(178.1)	(219.9)	(252.5)	(0.00407)	(0.00433)	(0.00468)	(0.00410)	(0.00417)	(0.00429)
	[−9,352––8,654]	[−5,936––5,074]	[−5,209––4,220]	[−0.0508––0.0349]	[−0.0473––0.0303]	[−0.0452––0.0269]	[−0.0193––0.00322]	[−0.0303––0.0140]	[−0.0340––0.0172]
TTD Duration Decile 6	−12,399***	−8,524***	−7,371***	−0.111***	−0.0952***	−0.0886***	−0.0637***	−0.0751***	−0.0763***
	(167.1)	(212.5)	(241.9)	(0.00420)	(0.00445)	(0.00470)	(0.00418)	(0.00417)	(0.00421)
	[−12,726––12,071]	[−8,941––8,108]	[−7,846––6,897]	[−0.119––0.103]	[−0.104––0.0865]	[−0.0978––0.0794]	[−0.0719––0.0555]	[−0.0833––0.0670]	[−0.0845––0.0680]

Table B.5—Continued

Variables	Annual Earnings: Difference from Control Workers			Employment: Difference from Control Workers			At-Injury Employment: Difference from Control Workers		
	First Post-Injury Year	Second Post-Injury Year	Third Post-Injury Year	Fourth Post-Injury Quarter	Eighth Post-Injury Quarter	Twelfth Post-Injury Quarter	Fourth Post-Injury Quarter	Eighth Post-Injury Quarter	Twelfth Post-Injury Quarter
TTD Duration Decile 7	-15,202***	-11,692***	-9,995***	-0.196***	-0.163***	-0.138***	-0.117***	-0.113***	-0.112***
	(170.4)	(206.4)	(234.4)	(0.00425)	(0.00448)	(0.00476)	(0.00418)	(0.00411)	(0.00413)
	[-15,535– -14,868]	[-12,097– -11,288]	[-10,454– -9,535]	[-0.204– -0.187]	[-0.172– -0.154]	[-0.147– -0.128]	[-0.126– -0.109]	[-0.121– -0.105]	[-0.120– -0.104]
TTD Duration Decile 8	-17,942***	-16,417***	-13,678***	-0.307***	-0.248***	-0.200***	-0.215***	-0.169***	-0.158***
	(176.0)	(211.3)	(238.3)	(0.00415)	(0.00436)	(0.00467)	(0.00413)	(0.00406)	(0.00405)
	[-18,287– -17,597]	[-16,831– -16,003]	[-14,145– -13,211]	[-0.315– -0.299]	[-0.256– -0.239]	[-0.210– -0.191]	[-0.223– -0.207]	[-0.177– -0.161]	[-0.166– -0.150]
TTD Duration Decile 9	-18,291***	-19,445***	-16,091***	-0.361***	-0.332***	-0.271***	-0.254***	-0.213***	-0.188***
	(173.1)	(203.9)	(235.1)	(0.00408)	(0.00426)	(0.00463)	(0.00409)	(0.00399)	(0.00400)
	[-18,630– -17,952]	[-19,845– -19,045]	[-16,552– -15,630]	[-0.369– -0.353]	[-0.340– -0.324]	[-0.280– -0.262]	[-0.262– -0.245]	[-0.220– -0.205]	[-0.196– -0.180]
TTD Duration Decile 10	-21,454***	-23,931***	-21,492***	-0.408***	-0.425***	-0.366***	-0.296***	-0.277***	-0.238***
	(188.5)	(219.0)	(241.4)	(0.00398)	(0.00402)	(0.00439)	(0.00402)	(0.00387)	(0.00391)
	[-21,823– -21,084]	[-24,361– -23,502]	[-21,965– -21,019]	[-0.415– -0.400]	[-0.433– -0.417]	[-0.374– -0.357]	[-0.304– -0.288]	[-0.285– -0.270]	[-0.246– -0.230]
Number of permanent impairments reported in WCIS Excluded group: No permanent impairments listed in WCIS									
1 Permanent Impairment Listed in WCIS	-302.6***	-789.0***	-1,501***	0.00897***	0.00415	-0.00413	0.0133***	0.0123***	0.00775***
	(112.4)	(138.6)	(158.1)	(0.00238)	(0.00255)	(0.00272)	(0.00242)	(0.00245)	(0.00248)
	[-523.0– -82.18]	[-1,061– -517.3]	[-1,811– -1,192]	[0.00430– 0.0136]	[-0.000850– -0.00916]	[-0.00946– 0.00119]	[0.00852– 0.0180]	[0.00753– 0.0171]	[0.00289– 0.0126]
2 Permanent Impairments Listed in WCIS	-560.4***	-1,281***	-2,020***	-0.00223	-0.0137***	-0.0263***	0.0124***	0.0115***	0.00425
	(145.9)	(179.6)	(205.2)	(0.00331)	(0.00351)	(0.00376)	(0.00334)	(0.00335)	(0.00340)
	[-846.4– -274.3]	[-1,633– -929.5]	[-2,422– -1,618]	[-0.00872– 0.00425]	[-0.0206– -0.00686]	[-0.0337– -0.0189]	[0.00591– 0.0190]	[0.00492– 0.0181]	[-0.00242– 0.0109]

Table B.5—Continued

Variables	Annual Earnings: Difference from Control Workers			Employment: Difference from Control Workers			At-Injury Employment: Difference from Control Workers		
	First Post-Injury Year	Second Post-Injury Year	Third Post-Injury Year	Fourth Post-Injury Quarter	Eighth Post-Injury Quarter	Twelfth Post-Injury Quarter	Fourth Post-Injury Quarter	Eighth Post-Injury Quarter	Twelfth Post-Injury Quarter
Site of injury on FROI									
Excluded group: 10 (Multiple head injury)									
FROI Injury Part of Body Code 11:Skull	1,366*	1,553	1,125	0.0371*	0.00740	0.0323	0.0437**	0.0329*	0.0300
	(791.2)	(963.0)	(1,088)	(0.0193)	(0.0204)	(0.0216)	(0.0193)	(0.0192)	(0.0185)
	[−184.8–2,917]	[−334.3–3,441]	[−1,008–3,259]	[−0.000856–0.0750]	[−0.0326–0.0474]	[−0.0101–0.0746]	[0.00586–0.0816]	[−0.00477–0.0706]	[−0.00618–0.0662]
FROI Injury Part of Body Code 12:Brain	−9,269***	−9,988***	−10,243***	−0.132***	−0.121***	−0.114***	−0.144***	−0.150***	−0.127***
	(882.5)	(1,100)	(1,161)	(0.0173)	(0.0188)	(0.0199)	(0.0171)	(0.0172)	(0.0166)
	[−10,998–−7,539]	[−12,144–−7,832]	[−12,519–−7,968]	[−0.166–−0.0980]	[−0.158–−0.0846]	[−0.153–−0.0755]	[−0.177–−0.110]	[−0.184–0.117]	[−0.159–−0.0941]
FROI Injury Part of Body Code 13:Ear(s)	4,908***	−4,990***	−7,245***	−0.00882	−0.0489***	−0.0362*	−0.00409	−0.0341**	−0.0221
	(1,059)	(1,325)	(1,463)	(0.0164)	(0.0174)	(0.0187)	(0.0165)	(0.0172)	(0.0173)
	[2,832–6,984]	[−7,587–−2,393]	[−10,114–−4,377]	[−0.0410–0.0234]	[−0.0830–−0.0148]	[−0.0728–0.000522]	[−0.0365–0.0283]	[−0.0678–−0.000497]	[−0.0559–0.0118]
FROI Injury Part of Body Code 14:Eye(s)	4,895***	4,691***	4,804***	0.0686***	0.0666***	0.0630***	0.0630***	0.0771***	0.0875***
	(713.1)	(892.4)	(1,005)	(0.0157)	(0.0173)	(0.0182)	(0.0158)	(0.0164)	(0.0158)
	[3,497–6,293]	[2,942–6,441]	[2,834–6,773]	[0.0379–0.0993]	[0.0327–0.100]	[0.0274–0.0987]	[0.0320–0.0940]	[0.0449–0.109]	[0.0565–0.118]
FROI Injury Part of Body Code 15:Nose	3,596***	3,094**	4,349**	0.0688**	0.0464	0.0948***	0.0609**	0.0427	0.0720**
	(1,240)	(1,483)	(1,756)	(0.0281)	(0.0302)	(0.0315)	(0.0283)	(0.0291)	(0.0287)
	[1,166–6,027]	[186.7–6,001]	[908.0–7,790]	[0.0137–0.124]	[−0.0127–0.106]	[0.0331–0.157]	[0.00535–0.116]	[−0.0142–0.0997]	[0.0157–0.128]
FROI Injury Part of Body Code 16:Teeth	7,484**	5,984	7,495	0.0733	0.0797	−0.000953	0.0511	0.0493	0.0545
	(3,321)	(4,916)	(4,854)	(0.0455)	(0.0507)	(0.0525)	(0.0439)	(0.0464)	(0.0543)
	[974.1–13,993]	[−3,652–15,620]	[−2,018–17,008]	[−0.0159–0.162]	[−0.0196–0.179]	[−0.104–0.102]	[−0.0349–0.137]	[−0.0416–0.140]	[−0.0518–0.161]

Table B.5—Continued

Variables	Annual Earnings: Difference from Control Workers			Employment: Difference from Control Workers			At-Injury Employment: Difference from Control Workers		
	First Post-Injury Year	Second Post-Injury Year	Third Post-Injury Year	Fourth Post-Injury Quarter	Eighth Post-Injury Quarter	Twelfth Post-Injury Quarter	Fourth Post-Injury Quarter	Eighth Post-Injury Quarter	Twelfth Post-Injury Quarter
FROI Injury Part of Body Code 17:Mouth	1,741	1,356	489.7	-0.0125	-0.00938	-0.0123	-0.0368	0.00644	-0.00818
	(1,682)	(2,165)	(2,555)	(0.0368)	(0.0399)	(0.0406)	(0.0350)	(0.0360)	(0.0362)
	[-1,557–5,038]	[-2,887–5,598]	[-4,519–5,498]	[-0.0846–0.0596]	[-0.0876–0.0689]	[-0.0919–0.0673]	[-0.105–0.0319]	[-0.0640–0.0769]	[-0.0792–0.0629]
FROI Injury Part of Body Code 18:Soft Tissue Head	1,093	1,430*	1,242	0.0351**	0.0257	0.0281	0.0389**	0.0323**	0.0342**
	(685.7)	(859.2)	(954.6)	(0.0156)	(0.0169)	(0.0178)	(0.0156)	(0.0158)	(0.0154)
	[-250.8–2,437]	[-254.4–3,114]	[-628.8–3,113]	[0.00458–0.0656]	[-0.00744–0.0589]	[-0.00674–0.0630]	[0.00830–0.0696]	[0.00124–0.0633]	[0.00403–0.0644]
FROI Injury Part of Body Code 19:Facial Bones	-1,350	-257.8	1,499	0.0908***	0.0612**	0.0657*	0.0621**	0.0556*	0.0759**
	(1,538)	(1,692)	(1,965)	(0.0293)	(0.0312)	(0.0353)	(0.0306)	(0.0300)	(0.0317)
	[-4,366–1,665]	[-3,574–3,058]	[-2,353–5,351]	[0.0334–0.148]	[5.49e-05–0.122]	[-0.00355–0.135]	[0.00211–0.122]	[-0.00322–0.114]	[0.0138–0.138]
FROI Injury Part of Body Code 20:Multiple Neck Injury	2,497***	1,236	1,416	0.0456***	0.0283*	0.0262	0.0561***	0.0410***	0.0413***
	(652.4)	(842.0)	(933.2)	(0.0144)	(0.0154)	(0.0164)	(0.0144)	(0.0146)	(0.0145)
	[1,218–3,775]	[-414.2–2,886]	[-413.3–3,245]	[0.0175–0.0738]	[-0.00189–0.0585]	[-0.00603–0.0584]	[0.0280–0.0842]	[0.0125–0.0695]	[0.0129–0.0698]
FROI Injury Part of Body Code 21:Vertebrae	502.5	-1,630	-1,051	-0.00914	-0.0218	-0.0180	0.0247	-0.00872	0.00654
	(968.7)	(1,109)	(1,344)	(0.0201)	(0.0214)	(0.0231)	(0.0205)	(0.0202)	(0.0208)
	[-1,396–2,401]	[-3,804–544.4]	[-3,686–1,583]	[-0.0485–0.0302]	[-0.0637–0.0201]	[-0.0632–0.0272]	[-0.0154–0.0649]	[-0.0484–0.0310]	[-0.0342–0.0473]
FROI Injury Part of Body Code 22:Disc	1,591**	-269.4	-271.8	0.0122	-0.00899	-0.00974	0.0144	0.00559	0.0105
	(706.3)	(893.1)	(1,074)	(0.0158)	(0.0168)	(0.0182)	(0.0157)	(0.0158)	(0.0157)
	[206.4–2,975]	[-2,020–1,481]	[-2,377–1,833]	[-0.0188–0.0431]	[-0.0419–0.0239]	[-0.0455–0.0260]	[-0.0162–0.0451]	[-0.0253–0.0365]	[-0.0204–0.0413]

Table B.5—Continued

Variables	Annual Earnings: Difference from Control Workers			Employment: Difference from Control Workers			At-Injury Employment: Difference from Control Workers		
	First Post-Injury Year	Second Post-Injury Year	Third Post-Injury Year	Fourth Post-Injury Quarter	Eighth Post-Injury Quarter	Twelfth Post-Injury Quarter	Fourth Post-Injury Quarter	Eighth Post-Injury Quarter	Twelfth Post-Injury Quarter
FROI Injury Part of Body Code 23:Spinal Cord	-2,027*	-1,130	-790.7	-0.0384	-0.00363	-0.00554	-0.0149	0.0106	0.0261
	(1,226)	(1,395)	(1,592)	(0.0266)	(0.0285)	(0.0318)	(0.0272)	(0.0265)	(0.0273)
	[-4,429–375.2]	[-3,864–1,603]	[-3,912–2,330]	[-0.0907–0.0138]	[-0.0596–0.0523]	[-0.0678–0.0567]	[-0.0681–0.0384]	[-0.0414–0.0627]	[-0.0273–0.0795]
FROI Injury Part of Body Code 24:Larynx	-209.4	-1,848	-6,658	-0.0137	0.00551	-0.0977	-0.0319	-0.0232	-0.0903
	(3,382)	(3,476)	(4,668)	(0.0609)	(0.0585)	(0.0767)	(0.0640)	(0.0618)	(0.0743)
	[-6,838–6,419]	[-8,660–4,965]	[-15,807–2,491]	[-0.133–0.106]	[-0.109–0.120]	[-0.248–0.0527]	[-0.157–0.0935]	[-0.144–0.0980]	[-0.236–0.0554]
FROI Injury Part of Body Code 25:Soft Tissue Neck	2,078***	-135.9	-792.4	0.00933	-0.00870	-0.00488	0.0233*	-0.00318	0.0122
	(584.8)	(744.3)	(818.8)	(0.0128)	(0.0139)	(0.0149)	(0.0128)	(0.0129)	(0.0129)
	[932.3–3,225]	[-1,595–1,323]	[-2,397–812.3]	[-0.0157–0.0344]	[-0.0359–0.0185]	[-0.0341–0.0243]	[-0.00181–0.0484]	[-0.0284–0.0221]	[-0.0130–0.0374]
FROI Injury Part of Body Code 26:Trachea	3,686	-4,935	-2,268	-0.0132	-0.122**	-0.0839	0.0239	-0.0397	-0.0457
	(2,852)	(4,291)	(5,542)	(0.0612)	(0.0606)	(0.0959)	(0.0644)	(0.0690)	(0.0977)
	[-1,904–9,276]	[-13,346–3,477]	[-13,130–8,594]	[-0.133–0.107]	[-0.241–0.00356]	[-0.272–0.104]	[-0.102–0.150]	[-0.175–0.0955]	[-0.237–0.146]
FROI Injury Part of Body Code 30:Multiple Upper Extremities	3,366***	1,571**	1,557**	0.0565***	0.0446***	0.0436***	0.0724***	0.0524***	0.0496***
	(512.0)	(644.5)	(717.0)	(0.0115)	(0.0125)	(0.0133)	(0.0115)	(0.0116)	(0.0114)
	[2,363–4,370]	[307.3–2,834]	[151.8–2,962]	[0.0340–0.0790]	[0.0202–0.0690]	[0.0174–0.0697]	[0.0500–0.0949]	[0.0297–0.0751]	[0.0273–0.0719]
FROI Injury Part of Body Code 31:Upper Arm (Excluding Clavicle & Scapula)	4,652***	5,141***	4,288***	0.104***	0.0901***	0.0891***	0.123***	0.107***	0.103***
	(543.1)	(694.0)	(781.1)	(0.0124)	(0.0135)	(0.0145)	(0.0125)	(0.0127)	(0.0126)
	[3,587–5,716]	[3,781–6,501]	[2,757–5,819]	[0.0798–0.128]	[0.0637–0.117]	[0.0606–0.118]	[0.0988–0.148]	[0.0821–0.132]	[0.0779–0.127]

Table B.5—Continued

Variables	Annual Earnings: Difference from Control Workers			Employment: Difference from Control Workers			At-Injury Employment: Difference from Control Workers		
	First Post-Injury Year	Second Post-Injury Year	Third Post-Injury Year	Fourth Post-Injury Quarter	Eighth Post-Injury Quarter	Twelfth Post-Injury Quarter	Fourth Post-Injury Quarter	Eighth Post-Injury Quarter	Twelfth Post-Injury Quarter
FROI Injury Part of Body Code 32:Elbow	4,981***	3,371***	3,685***	0.0957***	0.0696***	0.0759***	0.111***	0.0834***	0.0840***
	(530.8)	(676.7)	(754.0)	(0.0121)	(0.0131)	(0.0141)	(0.0121)	(0.0123)	(0.0122)
	[3,941–6,022]	[2,044–4,697]	[2,207–5,163]	[0.0720–0.119]	[0.0440–0.0953]	[0.0483–0.104]	[0.0874–0.135]	[0.0594–0.108]	[0.0601–0.108]
FROI Injury Part of Body Code 33:Lower Arm	4,653***	4,208***	4,194***	0.0942***	0.0829***	0.0733***	0.106***	0.0854***	0.0820***
	(514.6)	(658.2)	(732.1)	(0.0120)	(0.0130)	(0.0139)	(0.0119)	(0.0121)	(0.0119)
	[3,644–5,662]	[2,918–5,498]	[2,760–5,629]	[0.0708–0.118]	[0.0575–0.108]	[0.0460–0.101]	[0.0826–0.129]	[0.0617–0.109]	[0.0586–0.105]
FROI Injury Part of Body Code 34:Wrist	4,677***	3,905***	3,841***	0.0945***	0.0782***	0.0808***	0.106***	0.0879***	0.0845***
	(485.5)	(620.2)	(690.3)	(0.0110)	(0.0119)	(0.0128)	(0.0109)	(0.0111)	(0.0108)
	[3,726–5,629]	[2,690–5,121]	[2,488–5,194]	[0.0730–0.116]	[0.0548–0.102]	[0.0557–0.106]	[0.0849–0.128]	[0.0662–0.110]	[0.0633–0.106]
FROI Injury Part of Body Code 35:Hand	4,761***	3,293***	2,693***	0.0908***	0.0639***	0.0598***	0.0936***	0.0707***	0.0717***
	(489.8)	(622.9)	(694.7)	(0.0112)	(0.0121)	(0.0130)	(0.0112)	(0.0113)	(0.0111)
	[3,801–5,721]	[2,072–4,514]	[1,331–4,054]	[0.0689–0.113]	[0.0401–0.0876]	[0.0343–0.0853]	[0.0717–0.115]	[0.0485–0.0928]	[0.0499–0.0934]
FROI Injury Part of Body Code 36:Finger(s)	8,103***	8,224***	7,414***	0.180***	0.164***	0.143***	0.181***	0.170***	0.162***
	(483.9)	(616.1)	(684.8)	(0.0110)	(0.0121)	(0.0130)	(0.0111)	(0.0113)	(0.0111)
	[7,155–9,052]	[7,016–9,431]	[6,072–8,756]	[0.159–0.202]	[0.140–0.187]	[0.118–0.169]	[0.159–0.203]	[0.148–0.192]	[0.140–0.184]
FROI Injury Part of Body Code 37:Thumb	6,946***	5,469***	4,820***	0.132***	0.110***	0.105***	0.143***	0.109***	0.108***
	(570.6)	(739.2)	(819.5)	(0.0131)	(0.0143)	(0.0154)	(0.0132)	(0.0135)	(0.0136)
	[5,828–8,065]	[4,020–6,918]	[3,214–6,426]	[0.106–0.157]	[0.0821–0.138]	[0.0746–0.135]	[0.117–0.169]	[0.0829–0.136]	[0.0818–0.135]
FROI Injury Part of Body Code 38:Shoulder(s)	3,663***	4,224***	4,368***	0.0898***	0.0736***	0.0729***	0.105***	0.0897***	0.0867***
	(466.4)	(595.1)	(659.0)	(0.0105)	(0.0115)	(0.0123)	(0.0105)	(0.0106)	(0.0103)
	[2,749–4,577]	[3,058–5,391]	[3,076–5,660]	[0.0691–0.110]	[0.0511–0.0960]	[0.0488–0.0970]	[0.0846–0.126]	[0.0689–0.110]	[0.0665–0.107]

Table B.5—Continued

Variables	Annual Earnings: Difference from Control Workers			Employment: Difference from Control Workers			At-Injury Employment: Difference from Control Workers		
	First Post-Injury Year	Second Post-Injury Year	Third Post-Injury Year	Fourth Post-Injury Quarter	Eighth Post-Injury Quarter	Twelfth Post-Injury Quarter	Fourth Post-Injury Quarter	Eighth Post-Injury Quarter	Twelfth Post-Injury Quarter
FROI Injury Part of Body Code 39:Wrist(s) & Hand(s)	3,814*** (561.8) [2,713–4,915]	2,061*** (702.1) [685.0–3,437]	1,280 (780.2) [−249.4–2,809]	0.0626*** (0.0125) [0.0381–0.0871]	0.0557*** (0.0135) [0.0292–0.0821]	0.0399*** (0.0146) [0.0113–0.0684]	0.0792*** (0.0125) [0.0546–0.104]	0.0696*** (0.0127) [0.0447–0.0945]	0.0606*** (0.0125) [0.0360–0.0852]
FROI Injury Part of Body Code 40:Multiple Trunk	2,659*** (665.0) [1,356–3,963]	549.4 (835.6) [−1,088–2,187]	−944.3 (992.9) [−2,890–1,002]	0.0141 (0.0143) [−0.0140–0.0421]	0.00460 (0.0151) [−0.0250–0.0342]	−0.000202 (0.0162) [−0.0319–0.0315]	0.0125 (0.0141) [−0.0150–0.0401]	0.00970 (0.0140) [−0.0177–0.0371]	0.0165 (0.0138) [−0.0105–0.0435]
FROI Injury Part of Body Code 41:Upper Back Area (Thoracic Area)	1,575*** (519.2) [557.5–2,593]	1,041 (657.5) [−247.5–2,330]	1,474** (730.3) [42.19–2,905]	0.0211* (0.0116) [−0.00152–0.0438]	−0.00240 (0.0125) [−0.0268–0.0220]	0.00426 (0.0134) [−0.0220–0.0305]	0.0256** (0.0115) [0.00319–0.0481]	0.00476 (0.0116) [−0.0180–0.0276]	0.00867 (0.0114) [−0.0137–0.0311]
FROI Injury Part of Body Code 42:Lower Back Area (including Lumbar & Lumbo-Sacral)	853.1* (461.3) [−51.07–1,757]	−731.3 (586.5) [−1,881–418.3]	−1,065 (649.0) [−2,337–207.1]	−0.00798 (0.0104) [−0.0285–0.0125]	−0.0219* (0.0114) [−0.0442–0.000359]	−0.0178 (0.0122) [−0.0417–0.00597]	0.0104 (0.0104) [−0.00988–0.0308]	−0.00575 (0.0104) [−0.0262–0.0147]	−0.00125 (0.0101) [−0.0211–0.0186]
FROI Injury Part of Body Code 43:Disc	794.5 (807.1) [−787.4–2,376]	−903.2 (1,018) [−2,898–1,092]	−2,537** (1,270) [−5,027–−46.93]	−0.0145 (0.0191) [−0.0519–0.0229]	−0.0296 (0.0203) [−0.0695–0.0102]	−0.0288 (0.0228) [−0.0734–0.0158]	0.0154 (0.0190) [−0.0219–0.0527]	−0.00153 (0.0192) [−0.0392–0.0361]	0.00158 (0.0194) [−0.0365–0.0397]
FROI Injury Part of Body Code 44:Chest (including Ribs, Sternum & Soft Tissue)	1,199* (679.6) [−133.1–2,531]	812.5 (898.9) [−949.3–2,574]	−193.8 (981.8) [−2,118–1,730]	−0.0119 (0.0157) [−0.0428–0.0189]	−0.00713 (0.0168) [−0.0401–0.0258]	−0.0142 (0.0178) [−0.0491–0.0207]	0.0128 (0.0157) [−0.0180–0.0435]	0.00790 (0.0159) [−0.0232–0.0390]	0.0111 (0.0158) [−0.0198–0.0421]

Table B.5—Continued

Variables	Annual Earnings: Difference from Control Workers			Employment: Difference from Control Workers			At-Injury Employment: Difference from Control Workers		
	First Post-Injury Year	Second Post-Injury Year	Third Post-Injury Year	Fourth Post-Injury Quarter	Eighth Post-Injury Quarter	Twelfth Post-Injury Quarter	Fourth Post-Injury Quarter	Eighth Post-Injury Quarter	Twelfth Post-Injury Quarter
FROI Injury Part of Body Code 45:Sacrum and Coccyx	2,126*	633.3	1,158	0.0312	−0.0187	0.0148	0.0697**	0.0212	0.0181
	(1,141)	(1,387)	(1,865)	(0.0303)	(0.0324)	(0.0381)	(0.0321)	(0.0297)	(0.0315)
	[−111.3–4,363]	[−2,085–3,352]	[−2,497–4,813]	[−0.0282–0.0907]	[−0.0823–0.0448]	[−0.0598–0.0894]	[0.00676–0.133]	[−0.0371–0.0795]	[−0.0435–0.0797]
FROI Injury Part of Body Code 46:Pelvis	1,723	2,256	1,920	0.0346	0.0428	0.0324	0.0428	0.0578*	0.0522*
	(1,230)	(1,700)	(1,661)	(0.0303)	(0.0319)	(0.0327)	(0.0304)	(0.0299)	(0.0299)
	[−687.9–4,133]	[−1,076–5,589]	[−1,335–5,175]	[−0.0248–0.0941]	[−0.0198–0.105]	[−0.0316–0.0965]	[−0.0168–0.102]	[−0.000827–0.116]	[−0.00646–0.111]
FROI Injury Part of Body Code 47:Spinal Cord	972.5	−1,218	−224.7	0.00870	−0.0189	0.00514	0.00897	−0.0134	0.00405
	(1,142)	(1,503)	(1,732)	(0.0262)	(0.0269)	(0.0295)	(0.0257)	(0.0249)	(0.0257)
	[−1,265–3,210]	[−4,163–1,728]	[−3,619–3,169]	[−0.0427–0.0601]	[−0.0716–0.0339]	[−0.0526–0.0629]	[−0.0414–0.0594]	[−0.0622–0.0355]	[−0.0463–0.0544]
FROI Injury Part of Body Code 48:Internal Organs	−3,574***	−8,910***	−12,599***	−0.0962***	−0.109***	−0.126***	−0.0811***	−0.116***	−0.104***
	(1,220)	(1,537)	(1,692)	(0.0189)	(0.0203)	(0.0207)	(0.0190)	(0.0193)	(0.0189)
	[−5,965–−1,184]	[−11,923–−5,896]	[−15,915–−9,282]	[−0.133–−0.0592]	[−0.149–−0.0691]	[−0.167–−0.0856]	[−0.118–−0.0439]	[−0.154–−0.0782]	[−0.141–−0.0668]
FROI Injury Part of Body Code 49:Heart	−3,930***	−12,372***	−15,492***	−0.0523***	−0.114***	−0.127***	−0.0561***	−0.116***	−0.130***
	(1,178)	(1,578)	(1,685)	(0.0153)	(0.0171)	(0.0182)	(0.0155)	(0.0163)	(0.0166)
	[−6,238–−1,621]	[−15,464–−9,280]	[−18,795–−12,188]	[−0.0823–−0.0223]	[−0.148–−0.0808]	[−0.162–−0.0911]	[−0.0865–−0.0258]	[−0.148–−0.0844]	[−0.162–−0.0972]
FROI Injury Part of Body Code 50:Multiple Lower Extremities	2,123***	1,880**	1,930**	0.0656***	0.0256*	0.0369**	0.0715***	0.0380***	0.0435***
	(600.7)	(778.0)	(869.0)	(0.0140)	(0.0152)	(0.0163)	(0.0140)	(0.0143)	(0.0141)
	[945.8–3,300]	[355.7–3,405]	[226.3–3,633]	[0.0382–0.0931]	[−0.00423–0.0555]	[0.00509–0.0688]	[0.0440–0.0990]	[0.00995–0.0660]	[0.0158–0.0712]

Table B.5—Continued

Variables	Annual Earnings: Difference from Control Workers			Employment: Difference from Control Workers			At-Injury Employment: Difference from Control Workers		
	First Post-Injury Year	Second Post-Injury Year	Third Post-Injury Year	Fourth Post-Injury Quarter	Eighth Post-Injury Quarter	Twelfth Post-Injury Quarter	Fourth Post-Injury Quarter	Eighth Post-Injury Quarter	Twelfth Post-Injury Quarter
FROI Injury Part of Body Code 51:Hip	1,689**	2,466***	1,674*	0.0578***	0.0482***	0.0286*	0.0747***	0.0532***	0.0421***
	(695.5)	(841.0)	(920.0)	(0.0146)	(0.0156)	(0.0167)	(0.0146)	(0.0147)	(0.0146)
	[325.6–3,052]	[817.2–4,114]	[−128.9–3,477]	[0.0292–0.0864]	[0.0176–0.0789]	[−0.00414–0.0614]	[0.0462–0.103]	[0.0245–0.0819]	[0.0134–0.0708]
FROI Injury Part of Body Code 52:Upper Leg	3,629***	4,621***	4,737***	0.0827***	0.0702***	0.0718***	0.0833***	0.0755***	0.0883***
	(815.5)	(935.2)	(1,040)	(0.0170)	(0.0190)	(0.0196)	(0.0171)	(0.0176)	(0.0176)
	[2,031–5,227]	[2,788–6,454]	[2,698–6,776]	[0.0495–0.116]	[0.0330–0.107]	[0.0333–0.110]	[0.0498–0.117]	[0.0410–0.110]	[0.0537–0.123]
FROI Injury Part of Body Code 53:Knee	4,599***	5,973***	5,453***	0.115***	0.0989***	0.0895***	0.126***	0.114***	0.106***
	(465.6)	(593.7)	(658.5)	(0.0105)	(0.0114)	(0.0122)	(0.0104)	(0.0105)	(0.0102)
	[3,687–5,512]	[4,809–7,136]	[4,162–6,743]	[0.0944–0.135]	[0.0766–0.121]	[0.0656–0.113]	[0.106–0.147]	[0.0932–0.134]	[0.0862–0.126]
FROI Injury Part of Body Code 54:Lower Leg	2,976***	5,025***	5,297***	0.0775***	0.0695***	0.0610***	0.0845***	0.0857***	0.0875***
	(569.0)	(721.3)	(809.6)	(0.0129)	(0.0139)	(0.0148)	(0.0129)	(0.0130)	(0.0129)
	[1,861–4,091]	[3,611–6,438]	[3,710–6,883]	[0.0522–0.103]	[0.0423–0.0968]	[0.0320–0.0900]	[0.0592–0.110]	[0.0602–0.111]	[0.0623–0.113]
FROI Injury Part of Body Code 55:Ankle	3,810***	4,793***	4,214***	0.104***	0.0853***	0.0702***	0.112***	0.0949***	0.0878***
	(510.1)	(645.7)	(719.2)	(0.0116)	(0.0125)	(0.0135)	(0.0115)	(0.0117)	(0.0115)
	[2,811–4,810]	[3,527–6,059]	[2,805–5,624]	[0.0814–0.127]	[0.0607–0.110]	[0.0439–0.0966]	[0.0891–0.134]	[0.0720–0.118]	[0.0653–0.110]
FROI Injury Part of Body Code 56:Foot	3,221***	3,654***	3,010***	0.0851***	0.0605***	0.0561***	0.0921***	0.0756***	0.0835***
	(531.3)	(666.2)	(741.3)	(0.0121)	(0.0130)	(0.0140)	(0.0121)	(0.0122)	(0.0120)
	[2,179–4,262]	[2,348–4,960]	[1,557–4,463]	[0.0614–0.109]	[0.0350–0.0860]	[0.0286–0.0835]	[0.0684–0.116]	[0.0517–0.0994]	[0.0600–0.107]

Table B.5—Continued

Variables	Annual Earnings: Difference from Control Workers			Employment: Difference from Control Workers			At-Injury Employment: Difference from Control Workers		
	First Post-Injury Year	Second Post-Injury Year	Third Post-Injury Year	Fourth Post-Injury Quarter	Eighth Post-Injury Quarter	Twelfth Post-Injury Quarter	Fourth Post-Injury Quarter	Eighth Post-Injury Quarter	Twelfth Post-Injury Quarter
FROI Injury Part of Body Code 57:Toe(s)	4,960***	4,559***	4,112***	0.107***	0.0729***	0.0817***	0.118***	0.115***	0.101***
	(980.6)	(1,270)	(1,443)	(0.0224)	(0.0240)	(0.0255)	(0.0225)	(0.0228)	(0.0235)
	[3,038–6,882]	[2,071–7,048]	[1,285–6,940]	[0.0629–0.151]	[0.0259–0.120]	[0.0318–0.132]	[0.0735–0.162]	[0.0705–0.160]	[0.0547–0.147]
FROI Injury Part of Body Code 58:Great Toe	7,155***	7,785***	5,650***	0.127***	0.141***	0.112***	0.126***	0.127***	0.119***
	(1,611)	(1,725)	(1,795)	(0.0330)	(0.0345)	(0.0365)	(0.0338)	(0.0343)	(0.0345)
	[3,997–10,313]	[4,403–11,166]	[2,132–9,167]	[0.0625–0.192]	[0.0734–0.209]	[0.0408–0.184]	[0.0599–0.193]	[0.0597–0.194]	[0.0512–0.187]
FROI Injury Part of Body Code 60:Lungs	−876.6	−2,193	−2,315	−0.0331	−0.0464**	−0.0318	−0.0517**	−0.0715***	−0.0470**
	(1,067)	(1,359)	(1,589)	(0.0205)	(0.0217)	(0.0232)	(0.0204)	(0.0199)	(0.0193)
	[−2,969–1,215]	[−4,856–470.5]	[−5,430–799.3]	[−0.0733–0.00717]	[−0.0889–−0.00392]	[−0.0774–0.0137]	[−0.0916–−0.0118]	[−0.111–−0.0324]	[−0.0849–−0.00912]
FROI Injury Part of Body Code 61:Abdomen Including Groin	2,372***	1,327*	482.4	0.0293**	−0.00784	0.00129	0.0298**	0.00621	0.0157
	(609.5)	(771.1)	(855.2)	(0.0148)	(0.0157)	(0.0169)	(0.0148)	(0.0144)	(0.0143)
	[1,177–3,567]	[−184.1–2,839]	[−1,194–2,159]	[0.000422–0.0583]	[−0.0386–0.0229]	[−0.0318–0.0344]	[0.000768–0.0587]	[−0.0221–0.0345]	[−0.0122–0.0437]
FROI Injury Part of Body Code 62:Buttocks	2,280**	1,080	10.62	0.0240	−1.50e−05	−0.0230	0.0424	0.0286	0.0113
	(953.0)	(1,183)	(1,384)	(0.0272)	(0.0270)	(0.0298)	(0.0268)	(0.0255)	(0.0264)
	[411.7–4,147]	[−1,239–3,398]	[−2,703–2,724]	[−0.0293–0.0772]	[−0.0530–0.0529]	[−0.0814–0.0353]	[−0.0102–0.0950]	[−0.0213–0.0785]	[−0.0404–0.0631]
FROI Injury Part of Body Code 63:Lumbar and/or Sacral Vertebrae (Vertebrae NOC Trunk)	850.9	249.3	192.2	0.0123	0.00632	0.0143	0.0336**	0.0205	0.0353**
	(601.9)	(744.6)	(833.9)	(0.0144)	(0.0156)	(0.0168)	(0.0144)	(0.0145)	(0.0143)
	[−328.8–2,031]	[−1,210–1,709]	[−1,442–1,827]	[−0.0159–0.0405]	[−0.0243–0.0369]	[−0.0186–0.0471]	[0.00545–0.0617]	[−0.00801–0.0490]	[0.00725–0.0633]
FROI Injury Part of Body Code 64:Artificial Appliance	1,024	−158.6	43.47	−0.220	−0.110	−0.412***	−0.201	−0.0647	−0.00186
	(4,443)	(7,790)	(6,975)	(0.166)	(0.192)	(0.116)	(0.186)	(0.208)	(0.206)
	[−7,685–9,732]	[−15,427–15,110]	[−13,628–13,715]	[−0.544–0.105]	[−0.488–0.267]	[−0.640–−0.184]	[−0.565–0.164]	[−0.472–0.343]	[−0.405–0.401]

Table B.5—Continued

Variables	Annual Earnings: Difference from Control Workers			Employment: Difference from Control Workers			At-Injury Employment: Difference from Control Workers		
	First Post-Injury Year	Second Post-Injury Year	Third Post-Injury Year	Fourth Post-Injury Quarter	Eighth Post-Injury Quarter	Twelfth Post-Injury Quarter	Fourth Post-Injury Quarter	Eighth Post-Injury Quarter	Twelfth Post-Injury Quarter
FROI Injury Part of Body Code 65:Insufficient Info to Properly Identify—Unclassified	-1,837***	-2,769***	-1,284	-0.0642***	-0.0361**	-0.0139	-0.0698***	-0.0683***	-0.0422***
	(638.9)	(808.6)	(877.0)	(0.0143)	(0.0154)	(0.0165)	(0.0141)	(0.0139)	(0.0137)
	[-3,089– -584.8]	[-4,354– -1,184]	[-3,003– 434.9]	[-0.0922– -0.0362]	[-0.0663– -0.00597]	[-0.0462– 0.0184]	[-0.0973– -0.0422]	[-0.0955– -0.0411]	[-0.0691– -0.0154]
FROI Injury Part of Body Code 66:No Physical Injury	-10,158***	-10,888***	-10,195***	-0.155***	-0.118***	-0.100***	-0.190***	-0.187***	-0.160***
	(693.3)	(801.6)	(911.2)	(0.0135)	(0.0144)	(0.0154)	(0.0132)	(0.0130)	(0.0129)
	[-11,517– -8,799]	[-12,459– -9,317]	[-11,981– -8,409]	[-0.181– -0.128]	[-0.146– -0.0894]	[-0.130– -0.0699]	[-0.216– -0.164]	[-0.212– -0.161]	[-0.186– -0.135]
FROI Injury Part of Body Code 90:Multiple Body Parts	842.6*	-846.7	-957.4	0.00572	-0.00677	-0.00113	0.00790	-0.00766	0.00319
	(468.9)	(595.2)	(656.9)	(0.0105)	(0.0114)	(0.0122)	(0.0104)	(0.0105)	(0.0102)
	[-76.41– 1,762]	[-2,013– 319.7]	[-2,245– 330.2]	[-0.0148– 0.0262]	[-0.0291– 0.0155]	[-0.0250– 0.0227]	[-0.0124– 0.0282]	[-0.0282– 0.0129]	[-0.0168– 0.0231]
FROI Injury Part of Body Code 91:Body Systems and Multiple Body Systems	-8,606***	-9,480***	-8,801***	-0.152***	-0.118***	-0.103***	-0.178***	-0.181***	-0.150***
	(680.9)	(830.1)	(954.7)	(0.0145)	(0.0156)	(0.0166)	(0.0140)	(0.0139)	(0.0139)
	[-9,941– -7,272]	[-11,107– -7,853]	[-10,673– -6,930]	[-0.181– -0.124]	[-0.148– -0.0869]	[-0.136– -0.0704]	[-0.205– -0.150]	[-0.208– -0.154]	[-0.178– -0.123]
FROI Injury Part of Body Code 99:Whole Body	-7,596***	-9,749***	-8,153***	-0.123***	-0.0846**	-0.0585	-0.146***	-0.161***	-0.134***
	(1,793)	(2,393)	(2,432)	(0.0390)	(0.0389)	(0.0415)	(0.0348)	(0.0346)	(0.0344)
	[-11,110– -4,081]	[-14,439– -5,059]	[-12,921– -3,386]	[-0.200– -0.0468]	[-0.161– -0.00829]	[-0.140– 0.0227]	[-0.214– -0.0778]	[-0.229– -0.0930]	[-0.202– -0.0670]
Observations	327,610	327,611	304,260	327,610	327,644	304,293	327,610	327,644	304,293
R-squared	0.181	0.130	0.106	0.152	0.122	0.098	0.117	0.099	0.087

*** p < 0.01, ** p < 0.05, * p < 0.1

NOTES: Robust standard errors in parentheses. 95% confidence intervals in brackets. Outcome variables in regressions are differences between injured worker and control worker outcomes at selected post-injury time horizons; positive coefficients mean that higher values of the explanatory variables predict better outcomes for injured workers relative to controls. Regression models do not include time effects. Regression specifications are otherwise identical to those used for Tables B.5–B.7. Control variables not reported include pre-injury annual earnings (50 categories), gender, age, at-injury firm size, at-injury firm growth rate, at-injury firm separation rate, industry fixed effects, deciles of temporary disability duration, number of permanent impairments, and body part of injury.

Table B.6
Regression Coefficients for Firm Characteristics

Variables	Annual Earnings: Difference from Control Workers			Employment: Difference from Control Workers			At-Injury Employment: Difference from Control Workers		
	First Post-Injury Year	Second Post-Injury Year	Third Post-Injury Year	Fourth Post-Injury Quarter	Eighth Post-Injury Quarter	Twelfth Post-Injury Quarter	Fourth Post-Injury Quarter	Eighth Post-Injury Quarter	Twelfth Post-Injury Quarter
Firm size excluded group = 1–10 Employees									
Firm size 11–50 Employees	488.8	−27.98	−238.3	0.0241***	0.0197**	0.0162	0.0312***	0.0188**	0.0194*
	(389.7)	(430.6)	(474.5)	(0.00910)	(0.00969)	(0.0107)	(0.00939)	(0.00950)	(0.0100)
	[−274.9–1,253]	[−871.9–815.9]	[−1,168–691.8]	[0.00626–0.0419]	[0.000691–0.0387]	[−0.00471–0.0372]	[0.0128–0.0496]	[0.000140–0.0374]	[−0.000268–0.0391]
Firm size 51–100 Employees	976.8**	370.0	168.2	0.0518***	0.0414***	0.0355***	0.0592***	0.0380***	0.0372***
	(401.6)	(446.6)	(489.8)	(0.00940)	(0.00999)	(0.0110)	(0.00968)	(0.00974)	(0.0102)
	[189.6–1,764]	[−505.3–1,245]	[−791.7–1,128]	[0.0333–0.0702]	[0.0218–0.0610]	[0.0139–0.0570]	[0.0402–0.0782]	[0.0189–0.0571]	[0.0172–0.0573]
Firm size 101–500 Employees	1,085***	270.0	−34.43	0.0646***	0.0521***	0.0429***	0.0814***	0.0547***	0.0485***
	(380.7)	(418.4)	(457.4)	(0.00879)	(0.00936)	(0.0103)	(0.00907)	(0.00917)	(0.00970)
	[338.5–1,831]	[−550.0–1,090]	[−930.9–862.1]	[0.0474–0.0818]	[0.0338–0.0705]	[0.0227–0.0631]	[0.0636–0.0991]	[0.0368–0.0727]	[0.0295–0.0676]
Firm size 501–1000 Employees	1,357***	581.3	145.6	0.0776***	0.0587***	0.0525***	0.0956***	0.0642***	0.0597***
	(391.0)	(432.8)	(475.0)	(0.00901)	(0.00959)	(0.0106)	(0.00928)	(0.00939)	(0.00991)
	[591.0–2,124]	[−267.0–1,430]	[−785.4–1,077]	[0.0599–0.0952]	[0.0399–0.0775]	[0.0318–0.0732]	[0.0774–0.114]	[0.0458–0.0826]	[0.0403–0.0791]
Firm size 1001–5000 Employees	−452.4	−1,078**	−1,604***	0.0610***	0.0417***	0.0277***	0.0943***	0.0678***	0.0588***
	(382.2)	(421.8)	(461.9)	(0.00880)	(0.00937)	(0.0103)	(0.00908)	(0.00920)	(0.00973)
	[−1,202–296.8]	[−1,905–−251.5]	[−2,509–−698.9]	[0.0437–0.0782]	[0.0233–0.0600]	[0.00746–0.0479]	[0.0765–0.112]	[0.0497–0.0858]	[0.0398–0.0779]
Firm size 5001+ Employees	3,057***	2,502***	1,624***	0.114***	0.0915***	0.0685***	0.157***	0.133***	0.120***
	(382.2)	(424.8)	(467.8)	(0.00882)	(0.00939)	(0.0103)	(0.00909)	(0.00922)	(0.00975)
	[2,307–3,806]	[1,669–3,334]	[707.2–2,541]	[0.0968–0.131]	[0.0731–0.110]	[0.0482–0.0888]	[0.139–0.175]	[0.115–0.151]	[0.101–0.139]

Table B.6—Continued

Variables	Annual Earnings: Difference from Control Workers			Employment: Difference from Control Workers			At-Injury Employment: Difference from Control Workers		
	First Post-Injury Year	Second Post-Injury Year	Third Post-Injury Year	Fourth Post-Injury Quarter	Eighth Post-Injury Quarter	Twelfth Post-Injury Quarter	Fourth Post-Injury Quarter	Eighth Post-Injury Quarter	Twelfth Post-Injury Quarter
At-injury industry excluded group = Other industries									
Manufacturing	-443.9***	-641.6***	-402.9*	-0.0277***	-0.0359***	-0.0269***	-0.0240***	-0.0324***	-0.0298***
	(171.7)	(206.7)	(238.6)	(0.00362)	(0.00386)	(0.00418)	(0.00369)	(0.00374)	(0.00384)
	[-780.5 – -107.4]	[-1,047 – -236.4]	[-870.6 – 64.80]	[-0.0348 – -0.0206]	[-0.0435 – -0.0283]	[-0.0351 – -0.0187]	[-0.0312 – -0.0168]	[-0.0397 – -0.0251]	[-0.0373 – -0.0223]
Transportation/warehousing	-2,395***	1,112***	1,978***	-0.00361	0.0179***	0.0189***	0.00778	0.0239***	0.0275***
	(198.3)	(250.5)	(282.9)	(0.00473)	(0.00502)	(0.00546)	(0.00475)	(0.00477)	(0.00491)
	[-2,784 – -2,007]	[620.7 – 1,603]	[1,424 – 2,533]	[-0.0129 – 0.00565]	[0.00807 – 0.0277]	[0.00820 – 0.0296]	[-0.00154 – 0.0171]	[0.0146 – 0.0333]	[0.0179 – 0.0371]
Health care	-401.0**	86.25	418.1	-0.00860**	-0.0140***	-0.00313	-0.0130***	-0.0167***	-0.0115***
	(180.4)	(226.9)	(258.3)	(0.00396)	(0.00421)	(0.00462)	(0.00410)	(0.00416)	(0.00429)
	[-754.6 – -47.31]	[-358.5 – 531.0]	[-88.03 – 924.3]	[-0.0164 – -0.000827]	[-0.0222 – -0.00570]	[-0.0122 – 0.00592]	[-0.0210 – -0.00492]	[-0.0248 – -0.00854]	[-0.0199 – -0.00306]
Public administration	3,436***	2,118***	1,144***	0.0137***	-0.00130	-0.00611	0.0447***	0.0560***	0.0630***
	(230.7)	(287.7)	(327.9)	(0.00346)	(0.00378)	(0.00413)	(0.00358)	(0.00384)	(0.00407)
	[2,984 – 3,888]	[1,554 – 2,682]	[501.7 – 1,787]	[0.00691 – 0.0205]	[-0.00870 – 0.00609]	[-0.0142 – 0.00198]	[0.0377 – 0.0517]	[0.0485 – 0.0635]	[0.0550 – 0.0710]
Administrative/support	809.8***	2,206***	3,183***	0.0126***	0.0493***	0.0733***	-0.0111**	0.0176***	0.0369***
	(186.3)	(226.2)	(263.0)	(0.00486)	(0.00510)	(0.00550)	(0.00471)	(0.00453)	(0.00449)
	[444.7 – 1,175]	[1,763 – 2,650]	[2,667 – 3,698]	[0.00311 – 0.0221]	[0.0393 – 0.0593]	[0.0625 – 0.0841]	[-0.0203 – -0.00185]	[0.00872 – 0.0265]	[0.0281 – 0.0457]
Agriculture	1,413***	1,678***	1,944***	0.00434	0.0179**	0.0324***	0.00345	-0.00570	-2.18e-05
	(269.2)	(289.3)	(309.8)	(0.00708)	(0.00752)	(0.00823)	(0.00707)	(0.00704)	(0.00729)
	[885.9 – 1,941]	[1,111 – 2,245]	[1,336 – 2,551]	[-0.00954 – 0.0182]	[0.00317 – 0.0326]	[0.0163 – 0.0486]	[-0.0104 – 0.0173]	[-0.0195 – 0.00809]	[-0.0143 – 0.0143]

Table B.6—Continued

Variables	Annual Earnings: Difference from Control Workers			Employment: Difference from Control Workers			At-Injury Employment: Difference from Control Workers		
	First Post-Injury Year	Second Post-Injury Year	Third Post-Injury Year	Fourth Post-Injury Quarter	Eighth Post-Injury Quarter	Twelfth Post-Injury Quarter	Fourth Post-Injury Quarter	Eighth Post-Injury Quarter	Twelfth Post-Injury Quarter
Retail	-1,025*** (157.5) [-1,334 – -716.5]	-1,029*** (192.4) [-1,406 – -652.1]	-875.6*** (220.1) [-1,307 – -444.2]	-0.0334*** (0.00375) [-0.0407 – -0.0261]	-0.0470*** (0.00397) [-0.0547 – -0.0392]	-0.0535*** (0.00431) [-0.0619 – -0.0450]	-0.0313*** (0.00379) [-0.0387 – -0.0238]	-0.0441*** (0.00381) [-0.0516 – -0.0366]	-0.0538*** (0.00389) [-0.0614 – -0.0462]
Accommodations/food services	657.3*** (170.9) [322.3 – 992.3]	1,001*** (209.9) [589.9 – 1,413]	1,012*** (250.0) [521.8 – 1,502]	-0.00719 (0.00525) [-0.0175 – 0.00310]	-0.0115** (0.00552) [-0.0223 – -0.000704]	-0.0133** (0.00599) [-0.0250 – -0.00155]	-0.0245*** (0.00526) [-0.0349 – -0.0142]	-0.0337*** (0.00516) [-0.0438 – -0.0235]	-0.0399*** (0.00523) [-0.0502 – -0.0297]
Construction	-4,658*** (252.5) [-5,153 – -4,163]	-3,150*** (301.8) [-3,742 – -2,559]	-2,626*** (341.8) [-3,296 – -1,956]	-0.0551*** (0.00528) [-0.0654 – -0.0447]	-0.0365*** (0.00563) [-0.0475 – -0.0255]	-0.0297*** (0.00607) [-0.0416 – -0.0178]	-0.0444*** (0.00533) [-0.0549 – -0.0340]	-0.0256*** (0.00526) [-0.0359 – -0.0153]	-0.0246*** (0.00531) [-0.0350 – -0.0142]
Education	7,094*** (183.8) [6,734 – 7,455]	5,233*** (234.4) [4,774 – 5,693]	4,531*** (271.7) [3,999 – 5,064]	0.0996*** (0.00387) [0.0920 – 0.107]	0.0538*** (0.00431) [0.0454 – 0.0623]	0.0387*** (0.00473) [0.0294 – 0.0479]	0.0944*** (0.00400) [0.0866 – 0.102]	0.0700*** (0.00438) [0.0614 – 0.0786]	0.0705*** (0.00467) [0.0614 – 0.0797]
Wholesale	-795.4*** (220.8) [-1,228 – -362.6]	-1,187*** (275.2) [-1,727 – -648.1]	-1,196*** (316.3) [-1,816 – -575.8]	-0.0362*** (0.00501) [-0.0460 – -0.0264]	-0.0337*** (0.00534) [-0.0442 – -0.0233]	-0.0329*** (0.00580) [-0.0443 – -0.0215]	-0.0326*** (0.00517) [-0.0427 – -0.0224]	-0.0406*** (0.00519) [-0.0508 – -0.0305]	-0.0446*** (0.00536) [-0.0551 – -0.0341]
Firm annual employment growth excluded group = below -30%									
Firm Annual Growth Rate (-30% to -10%)	-1,676*** (324.8) [-2,312 – -1,039]	-1,660*** (377.2) [-2,400 – -921.1]	-1,738*** (417.7) [-2,556 – -919.0]	-0.0488*** (0.00785) [-0.0641 – -0.0334]	-0.0486*** (0.00825) [-0.0648 – -0.0324]	-0.0584*** (0.00872) [-0.0755 – -0.0413]	-0.0420*** (0.00762) [-0.0570 – -0.0271]	-0.0389*** (0.00736) [-0.0533 – -0.0244]	-0.0413*** (0.00717) [-0.0554 – -0.0273]

Table B.6—Continued

Variables	Annual Earnings: Difference from Control Workers			Employment: Difference from Control Workers			At-Injury Employment: Difference from Control Workers		
	First Post-Injury Year	Second Post-Injury Year	Third Post-Injury Year	Fourth Post-Injury Quarter	Eighth Post-Injury Quarter	Twelfth Post-Injury Quarter	Fourth Post-Injury Quarter	Eighth Post-Injury Quarter	Twelfth Post-Injury Quarter
Firm annual growth rate (−10% to −0.5%)	−2,572*** (318.7) [−3,196– −1,947]	−2,904*** (370.2) [−3,630– −2,178]	−3,371*** (411.2) [−4,177– −2,565]	−0.0574*** (0.00761) [−0.0723– −0.0425]	−0.0710*** (0.00802) [−0.0867– −0.0553]	−0.0930*** (0.00848) [−0.110– −0.0764]	−0.0439*** (0.00739) [−0.0584– −0.0294]	−0.0479*** (0.00716) [−0.0619– −0.0338]	−0.0543*** (0.00697) [−0.0679– −0.0406]
Firm annual growth rate (−0.5% to 0.5%)	−2,208*** (353.6) [−2,901– −1,515]	−2,646*** (414.1) [−3,458– −1,834]	−3,433*** (462.5) [−4,340– −2,527]	−0.0590*** (0.00830) [−0.0753– −0.0428]	−0.0669*** (0.00879) [−0.0841– −0.0497]	−0.0939*** (0.00932) [−0.112– −0.0757]	−0.0444*** (0.00815) [−0.0604– −0.0284]	−0.0429*** (0.00802) [−0.0587– −0.0272]	−0.0525*** (0.00795) [−0.0681– −0.0369]
Firm annual growth rate (0.5% to 10%)	−2,647*** (321.1) [−3,277– −2,018]	−3,077*** (372.6) [−3,807– −2,346]	−3,712*** (414.7) [−4,525– −2,899]	−0.0704*** (0.00766) [−0.0854– −0.0553]	−0.0815*** (0.00807) [−0.0973– −0.0657]	−0.105*** (0.00853) [−0.122– −0.0885]	−0.0514*** (0.00744) [−0.0659– −0.0368]	−0.0517*** (0.00721) [−0.0658– −0.0376]	−0.0588*** (0.00703) [−0.0726– −0.0450]
Firm annual growth rate (10% to 30%)	(335.2) [−3,909– −2,595]	−3,252*** (386.5) [−4,408– −2,893]	−3,650*** (427.7) [−4,966– −3,289]	−4,127*** (0.00791) [−0.0833– −0.0524]	−0.0679*** (0.00832) [−0.0913– −0.0586]	−0.0749*** (0.00881) [−0.112– −0.0775]	−0.0947*** (0.00770) [−0.0686– −0.0384]	−0.0535*** (0.00745) [−0.0636– −0.0343]	−0.0489*** (0.00728) [−0.0682– −0.0396]
Firm annual growth rate (30%+)	−2,706*** (355.0) [−3,401– −2,010]	−2,087*** (411.8) [−2,895– −1,280]	−2,164*** (460.1) [−3,066– −1,262]	−0.0374*** (0.00843) [−0.0539– −0.0209]	−0.0229*** (0.00886) [−0.0402– −0.00552]	−0.0326*** (0.00941) [−0.0511– −0.0142]	−0.0317*** (0.00817) [−0.0478– −0.0157]	−0.0121 (0.00786) [−0.0275– 0.00325]	−0.00997 (0.00769) [−0.0250– 0.00509]
Firm separation rate Excluded Category: Separation rate below 4.4%									
Firm separation rate Quartile 2 (4.4% to 8.1%)	−938.4*** (148.4) [−1,229– −647.6]	−330.0* (183.0) [−688.6– 28.70]	−210.5 (212.9) [−627.9– 206.9]	−0.00731*** (0.00271) [−0.0126– −0.00200]	0.000358 (0.00294) [−0.00540– 0.00612]	0.00427 (0.00323) [−0.00207– 0.0106]	−0.0181*** (0.00281) [−0.0236– −0.0126]	−0.0225*** (0.00299) [−0.0283– −0.0166]	−0.0275*** (0.00319) [−0.0337– −0.0212]

Table B.6—Continued

Variables	Annual Earnings: Difference from Control Workers			Employment: Difference from Control Workers			At-Injury Employment: Difference from Control Workers		
	First Post-Injury Year	Second Post-Injury Year	Third Post-Injury Year	Fourth Post-Injury Quarter	Eighth Post-Injury Quarter	Twelfth Post-Injury Quarter	Fourth Post-Injury Quarter	Eighth Post-Injury Quarter	Twelfth Post-Injury Quarter
Firm separation rate Quartile 3 (8.1% to 14.1%)	-1,060***	-366.4*	-59.65	-0.0178***	-0.000474	0.00629*	-0.0352***	-0.0302***	-0.0299***
	(154.2)	(193.3)	(222.9)	(0.00314)	(0.00338)	(0.00371)	(0.00324)	(0.00338)	(0.00355)
	[-1,362– -757.4]	[-745.2– 12.44]	[-496.5– 377.2]	[-0.0240– -0.0117]	[-0.00711– 0.00616]	[-0.000984– 0.0136]	[-0.0416– -0.0289]	[-0.0368– -0.0235]	[-0.0368– -0.0229]
Firm separation rate quartile 4 (14.1%+)	-460.9***	1,134***	1,661***	0.00922**	0.0429***	0.0556***	-0.0289***	-0.00432	0.00966**
	(173.4)	(214.2)	(244.2)	(0.00375)	(0.00402)	(0.00439)	(0.00384)	(0.00393)	(0.00408)
	[-800.7– -121.0]	[714.4– 1,554]	[1,182– 2,139]	[0.00187– 0.0166]	[0.0351– 0.0508]	[0.0470– 0.0642]	[-0.0364– -0.0213]	[-0.0120– 0.00338]	[0.00166– 0.0177]
Observations	327,610	327,611	304,260	327,610	327,644	304,293	327,610	327,644	304,293
R-squared	0.181	0.130	0.106	0.152	0.122	0.098	0.117	0.099	0.087

NOTE: Robust standard errors in parentheses. 95% confidence intervals in brackets. Outcome variables in regressions are differences between injured worker and control worker outcomes at selected post-injury time horizons: positive coefficients mean that higher values of the explanatory variables predict better outcomes for injured workers relative to controls. Regression models do not include time effects. Regression specifications are otherwise identical to those used for Tables B.5–B.7. Control variables not reported include pre-injury annual earnings (50 categories), gender, age, at-injury firm size, at-injury firm growth rate, at-injury firm separation rate, industry fixed effects, deciles of temporary disability duration, number of permanent impairments, and body part of injury.

*** p < 0.01, ** p < 0.05, * p < 0.1

Table B.6 reports the effects of firm characteristics on outcomes for injured workers. All regressions also control for quarterly time effects and 50 bins of real pre-injury earnings.

Effect of Economic Conditions on Losses

Our regression estimates show that there was a substantial decrease in relative earnings for disabled workers who were injured during and after the Great Recession, even after including a rich set of control variables measuring characteristics of the worker, the at-injury job, and the nature and severity of the injury. To evaluate the influence of economic conditions more directly, we modified the regression model used for case-mix adjustment by replacing time effects with measures of economic conditions at the time of injury:

$$y_{ijqt}^I - y_{ijqt}^C = f(E^{I,\text{pre-injury}}, \beta^E) + EP^{\text{state}}\beta^{\text{state}} + \%\Delta_{t-04}EP^{\text{industry}}\beta^{\text{ind}}$$
$$+ X_i^D\beta^D + X_i^I\beta^I + X_{jq}^F\beta^F + \varepsilon_{ijqt}$$

where

EP^{state} is the statewide employment-population ratio for 18- to 64-year-olds in the quarter of injury. A one-unit change corresponds to a 1 percentage point increase in the number of jobs per adult in California.[5]

$\%\Delta_{t-04}EP^{\text{industry}}$ is the percentage change relative to 2004 in the employment-population ratio for the industry of the at-injury firm, where the 2004 baseline is from the same calendar quarter as the quarter of injury to control for seasonality in industry-specific employment. A one-unit change corresponds to a 1 percent increase over 2004 in industry employment relative to the statewide adult population. Scaling $\%\Delta_{t-04}EP^{\text{industry}}$ as an index where the 2004 level is equal to 100 for all industries allows us to compare changes in employment across industries of dramatically different sizes while normalizing for population growth.

EP^{state} captures the overall condition of the statewide labor market in the quarter of injury, while $\%\Delta_{t-04}EP^{\text{industry}}$ captures the level of labor demand in the at-injury industry in the quarter of injury. The regression model controls for all other case-mix adjusters described above, including the firm-level rate of year-on-year employment growth at the time of injury and the turnover rate. Because these two time-varying firm characteristics directly control for changes in labor demand and the probability of job separation at the at-injury employer, EP^{state} and $\%\Delta_{t-04}EP^{\text{industry}}$ should be interpreted as reflecting the impact of broader economic conditions on outcomes for disabled workers independently of hiring and firing at the at-injury employer. Among other things, $\%\Delta_{t-04}EP^{\text{industry}}$ may capture labor demand at other firms in the same industry, while EP^{state} may capture labor demand in different industries.

Table B.7 reports the regression coefficients for EP^{state} and $\%\Delta_{t-04}EP^{\text{industry}}$ in regressions for earnings and employment outcomes at one, two, and three years post-injury. (All other worker, injury, and firm characteristics, including the time-varying firm characteristics, have very similar effects on injured worker outcomes to the coefficients presented above in Tables B.4 to B.6.) Post-injury annual earnings for injured workers are significantly higher when the state-

---

[5]   We used total UI-covered employment from the BLS QCEW as the nominator for our employment-to-population ratio and Census Bureau population estimates of the 18- to 64-year-old population as our denominator. While changes in the age structure of employment above age 64 could generate spurious variation in this measure, we believe that this employment-to-population ratio is adequate as a rough proxy for economic conditions.

Table B.7
Effect of Statewide and Industry Employment/Population Ratios on Earnings Losses

	Annual Earnings: Difference from Control Workers			Employment: Difference from Control Workers			At-Injury Employment: Difference from Control Workers		
	First Post-Injury Year	Second Post-Injury Year	Third Post-Injury Year	End of First Post-Injury Year (QOI+4)	End of Second Post-Injury Year (QOI+8)	End of Third Post-Injury Year (QOI+12)	End of First Post-Injury Year (QOI+4)	End of Second Post-Injury Year (QOI+8)	End of Third Post-Injury Year (QOI+12)
Statewide employment/ population ratio	271.4***	230.4***	154.5***	0.00593***	0.00378***	0.000564	0.00813***	0.00862***	0.00826***
	(13.54)	(16.83)	(19.26)	(0.000306)	(0.000326)	(0.000357)	(0.000309)	(0.000312)	(0.000322)
	[244.9–298.0]	[197.4–263.3]	[116.8–192.3]	[0.00533–0.00653]	[0.00314–0.00442]	[−0.000135–0.00126]	[0.00752–0.00873]	[0.00801–0.00923]	[0.00763–0.00889]
% change from 2004 in at-injury industry employment/population ratio	−45.02***	−15.91*	−1.503	0.000163	0.000499**	0.000696***	−0.000365*	−0.000466**	−0.000298
	(7.618)	(9.034)	(10.58)	(0.000187)	(0.000198)	(0.000226)	(0.000188)	(0.000181)	(0.000187)
	[−59.95–−30.09]	[−33.62–1.792]	[−22.25–19.24]	[−0.000205–0.000530]	[0.000111–0.000888]	[0.000253–0.00114]	[−0.000735–3.92e−06]	[−0.000821–−0.000111]	[−0.000664–6.75e−05]
Observations	327,520	327,521	304,177	327,520	327,554	304,210	327,520	327,554	304,210
R-squared	0.178	0.126	0.104	0.149	0.119	0.096	0.115	0.097	0.086

NOTES: Outcome variables in regressions are differences between injured worker and control worker outcomes at selected post-injury time horizons: positive coefficients mean that higher values of the explanatory variables predict better outcomes for injured workers relative to controls. Regression models do not include time effects. Regression specifications are otherwise identical to those used for Tables B.5–B.7. Control variables not reported include pre-injury annual earnings (50 categories), gender, age, at-injury firm size, at-injury firm growth rate, at-injury firm separation rate, industry fixed effects, deciles of temporary disability duration, number of permanent impairments, and body part of injury. *** $p < 0.01$, ** $p < 0.05$, * $p < 0.1$

wide employment-to-population ratio is higher, implying that a 1-percentage-point decrease in employment-to-population predicts a decrease of $230 in annual earnings in the second post-injury year. To place this in context, we may note that, between 2005 and 2012, the statewide employment-to-population ratio peaked at 68.1 percent in 2006–2007 and reached a trough of 60.6 percent in 2011, leading to a predicted $1,728 reduction in injured worker earnings in the second post-injury year. However, the impact of overall economic conditions on post-injury earnings declines in magnitude over the first three post-injury years, and the same pattern is apparent with the impact on injured worker employment (which shrinks and becomes statistically insignificantly different from zero by the third post-injury year).

The impact of industry-specific employment-to-population on earnings loss is much less pronounced and is essentially zero after the first post-injury year.[6] It is notable that injured worker employment becomes significantly associated with industry-specific employment-to-population in the second and third post-injury years (on the time scale when the impact of statewide employment is decaying), but the magnitude of this effect appears to be much smaller than the effect of statewide employment.

There is a fundamental limitation inherent in this modeling approach, which is that we can estimate the impact of statewide economic conditions on earnings and employment losses only under the assumption that other time-varying factors do not affect earnings and employment losses. Even though we control for a rich set of other variables, this assumption is likely too strong to be realistic. In particular, these results do not substantiate the conclusion that changes in economic conditions *caused* the dramatic increases in earnings losses observed following the Great Recession unless we are willing to assume that no other time-varying factors influenced outcomes for disabled workers. What we do learn from this model, and from the estimates of relative earnings presented in Figure 4.9, is the extent to which the case-mix-adjusted time profile of earnings loss during the 2005–2012 period could be predicted purely using injury characteristics and economic conditions. Unsurprisingly, the model using economic conditions captures the drop in relative earnings associated with the Great Recession as well as the slow recovery.

While it is impossible to test the assumption that time-varying factors other than economic conditions caused the decline in relative earnings observed between 2005 and 2012, we can perform a statistical test to compare the fit of the case-mix-adjusted model with flexible time effects to the model that controls for statewide economic conditions. Specifically, we used the P-test for non-nested regression models described in Davidson and MacKinnon (1993). This is a test of the null hypothesis that one model is the true model against the alternative hypothesis that a competing, non-nested model is true.[7] We perform the test twice, once to test the model with time effects and once to test the model with employment rates. The model with employment rates is strongly rejected ($p < 0.001$), but the model with time effects is only marginally rejected ($p = 0.075$), indicating that employment rates fail to capture information about earnings losses that is not absorbed in the time effects. Time effects are perfectly collinear with statewide employment rates, so this is not entirely surprising, as the model with time effects is more flexible in terms of modeling statewide economic conditions.

---

[6]   The change in the average level across industries of $\%\Delta_{t-04}EP^{\text{industry}}$ between the peak and the trough of the business cycle is about 9.2 percentage points, and the range between the 10th and 90th percentile in any year varies between roughly 5 and 10 percentage points.

[7]   The test can be implemented by including the fitted value from the competing model in the model assumed under the null and conducting a t-test on the coefficient for the fitted value.

Alternative Specification To examine the robustness of our estimates to functional form, we also estimated all regression models using an alternative specification in which the dependent variable is the level of the injured worker's post-injury outcome (earnings, employment, or at-injury employment). Instead of using the difference between injured worker and control worker outcomes as the dependent variable (as in our main model), this model includes the control worker's post-injury outcomes and the injured worker's pre-injury outcomes as explanatory variables. This specification, which is similar to the models used in earlier RAND studies, has the slight disadvantage that the model has to explain idiosyncratic variation in the level of the injured worker's outcome rather than differencing out this variation. However, inclusion of the matched control outcome as an explanatory variable means that this difference may be small in practice.

$$y_{ijqt}^{I} = f(E^{I,\text{pre-injury}}, \beta^{E}) + f(y_{ijqt}^{C}, \beta^{C}) + X_{i}^{D}\beta^{D} + X_{i}^{I}\beta^{I} + X_{jq}^{F}\beta^{F} + \mu_{q} + \varepsilon_{ijqt}$$

Estimates of the impact of case-mix adjusters on injured worker earnings were very similar to those obtained from our preferred (differenced) model and are not reported here.

Specification for Proportional Losses Neither our preferred specification nor the alternative model is well suited to estimating relative earnings or relative employment. The problem is that these models do not explicitly model control worker outcomes, which are the denominator of relative earnings. Previous RAND studies have fixed control worker outcomes at overall sample averages. It is highly likely that control worker outcomes vary systematically with characteristics of interest, meaning that relative outcomes estimated using a sample average may be biased. As discussed above, it is not feasible to calculate relative earnings prior to taking averages or fitting regression models because injured workers whose controls have zeroes or very low values for the outcomes lead to outliers and missing data when relative outcomes are calculated at the individual level. We therefore sought to find a middle ground between using the same denominator for all workers in a quarter of injury and modeling individual-level relative earnings.

To generate the figures illustrating relative outcomes in this report, we used a third regression specification that estimates separate linear regression models for injured worker and control worker outcomes.

$$y_{ijqt}^{I} = f(E^{I,\text{pre-injury}}, \beta^{E}) + X_{i}^{D}\beta^{D} + X_{i}^{I}\beta^{I} + X_{jq}^{F}\beta^{F} + \mu_{q} + \varepsilon_{ijqt}^{I}$$

$$y_{ijqt}^{C} = f(E^{I,\text{pre-injury}}, \gamma^{E}) + X_{i}^{D}\gamma^{D} + X_{i}^{I}\gamma^{I} + X_{jq}^{F}\gamma^{F} + \nu_{q} + \varepsilon_{ijqt}^{C}$$

These models allow us to calculate predicted values for both control and injured worker outcomes for all individuals in our population. We then take the ratio of these predicted values as our measure of relative outcomes. This captures systematic variation in both injured and control worker outcomes that is correlated with our explanatory variables of interest while aggregating the data sufficiently to avoid the problems caused by infinitesimal or zero outcomes for the control workers. It also has the benefit of allowing us to distinguish the roles of injured worker and control worker outcomes in our estimates of the impact of injury. That said, the regression models used to estimate relative outcomes have the drawback that they do not fully exploit the availability of matched controls, since injured workers are not explicitly paired with their control workers except for purposes of statistical inference.

To calculate regression-adjusted effects of an explanatory variable of interest, we fixed all other covariates at their sample averages and then varied the variable of interest to calculate predicted injured and control worker earnings as a function of the variable of interest. Calculating predicted values for the control workers solves the problems of outliers and missing data by effectively averaging out zeroes and small positive values.[8] For example, to calculate the regression-adjusted time trends in Figure 4.4 we constructed the fitted values

$$\hat{y}^I(q) = \overline{f(E^{I,\text{pre-injury}},\hat{\beta}^E)} + \overline{X}_i^D\hat{\beta}^D + \overline{X}_i^I\hat{\beta}^I + \overline{X}_{jq}^F\hat{\beta}^F + \mu_q$$
$$\hat{y}^C(q) = \overline{f(E^{I,\text{pre-injury}},\hat{\gamma}^E)} + \overline{X}_i^D\hat{\gamma}^D + \overline{X}_i^I\hat{\gamma}^I + \overline{X}_{jq}^F\hat{\gamma}^F + \nu_q$$

We then define regression-adjusted relative earnings in quarter q as

$$\text{Regression-Adjusted Relative Earnings for Quarter } q = \frac{\hat{y}^I(q)}{\hat{y}^C(q)}$$

For Figure 4.9, we use the same approach to calculate predicted values for the model that uses employment-to-population ratios in place of time effects, fixing all other variables at sample averages while varying the economic conditions variables. Because the industry-specific employment-to-population measure $\%\Delta_{t-04}EP^{\text{industry}}$ varies across observations at a point in time, we use the actual distribution of at-injury industry in each quarter to construct a weighted average of $\%\Delta_{t-04}EP^{\text{industry}}$. Standard errors are calculated using the delta method to account for sampling uncertainty in our estimates of the variable of interest. We ignore sampling uncertainty in the other regression parameters because we are only using these estimates to determine the appropriate level of the response function of y with respect to the variable of interest. This could be calculated just as easily using the overall sample average of y, which has infinitesimal standard errors because our sample is very large. The separate regression models here are estimated as seemingly unrelated regressions so that the residual correlation between outcomes for injured workers and their matched controls (formally, the error terms ε_{ijqt}^I and ε_{ijqt}^C) is accounted for. This correlation is fairly strong (e.g., $\rho = 0.18$ for earnings in the second post-injury year) because our sample is matched.

The drawback of using separate regression models to estimate the effects of covariates on injured and control worker earnings is that this specification does not make efficient use of our matched sample: injured workers are not explicitly compared to their matched controls at the individual level. We therefore view the differenced regression specification as the most accurate estimate of the impact of covariates on outcomes. It is reported in this appendix so that readers can confirm that the estimated impacts of covariates are qualitatively very similar across models.

The fact that the differenced model and the model estimated in levels yield similar results should not be viewed as evidence that the selection of matched controls is not methodologically important. It might, in fact, be argued that the stability of our estimates across very different models is evidence for the success of the matching procedure in eliminating bias due

---

[8]   Although our use of linear models for binary outcomes could potentially create problems with predicted probabilities below zero or greater than 100 percent, this is less of a concern for our purposes because we are interested in predictions near the sample average. In practice, our predicted probabilities were all reasonable and well-behaved.

Table B.8
Decomposition Results, 2010–2012 Versus 2005–2007

Share of Change Explained by . . .	Average % Earnings Loss	Median % Earnings Loss	Average % Reduction in Employment
Time effects	55	64	59
Compositional effects	45	36	41

Table B.9
Detailed Decomposition Results for Change in Average Earnings and Employment, 2008–2012 Versus 2005–2007

Group of Variables	Relative Earnings (%)	Relative Employment (%)
Injury severity	−1.31 (0.12)	−0.91 (0.08)
Pre-injury wage	−0.78 (0.05)	−0.56 (0.03)
Separation rate	−0.76 (0.08)	−0.26 (0.04)
Age at Injury	−0.58 (0.03)	−0.54 (0.03)
Firm size	−0.41 (0.05)	−0.37 (0.04)
Gender	−0.08 (0.02)	0.01 (0.01)
Industry	0.29 (0.09)	0.19 (0.05)
Growth rate	0.58 (0.09)	0.42 (0.06)
Job tenure	0.51 (0.04)	−0.15 (0.02)

NOTES: Table reports detailed Oaxaca-Blinder decomposition results for second-year relative earnings and employment 8 quarters post-injury. Standard errors in parentheses.

to unobservable heterogeneity (Ho et al., 2007). There is no guarantee that this stability would hold in a sample that had not been carefully pre-selected so that injured and uninjured workers have the same pre-injury earnings potential.

Methods for Decomposition of Changes in Average Outcomes

To quantify the contribution of compositional changes to the overall change in outcomes associated with the Great Recession, we estimate Oaxaca-Blinder decompositions for the change in proportional earnings loss between the pre-recession period and the post-recession period. We use a modified version of individual-level relative earnings as the outcome variable, in which post-injury control wages are averaged over 50 cells of pre-injury earnings in each quarter of injury. The averaging ensures that the denominator of relative earnings is positive and not excessively small for all injured workers. Construction of this modified individual-level variable allows us to focus on a single outcome for the Oaxaca-Blinder decomposition here.

To assess robustness, we also estimate a DeNardo-Fortin-Lemeiux median decomposition for relative earnings. Finally, we estimate an Oaxaca-Blinder decomposition for the difference between (binary) injured worker employment and average control worker employment, which can be modeled as a continuous (if bunched and highly non-normal) variable. The median decomposition and the decomposition of employment should not be affected by outliers in relative earnings, which may still be a concern even though we average control worker wages before calculating relative earnings. Table 4.6 in the text presents results comparing outcomes after the start of the recession (2008–2012) to pre-recession (2005–2007) outcomes. Table B.8 reports similar calculations that omit the recession years from the sample, comparing 2010–2012 to 2005–2007. The estimated contribution of compositional effects is slightly smaller, by 2 percentage points for average earnings loss, 1 percentage point for the median, and 2 percentage points for the reduction in employment. All our decompositions use pre-recession coefficients to calculate the impact of changes in endowment. Table B.9 presents detailed decomposition results for the Oaxaca-Blinder decompositions underlying Table 4.6. These estimates may be of interest to readers wishing to understand which compositional factors were most important in explaining the increase in losses over time.

Robustness of Earnings Loss Trends to Outliers and Differential Non-Reporting of Injuries

Effect of Outliers on Earnings Loss Estimates

Our main results primarily rely on estimates of average earnings and wage loss. Averages can be very sensitive to outliers, and so we defined a maximum level of quarterly earnings as a criterion for inclusion in our analysis sample. Our main estimates treat workers with quarterly earnings in any quarter of their wage histories above $250,000 (so annual earnings above $1 million) as outliers. This threshold leads to exclusion of 189 otherwise eligible individuals (0.05 percent of the sample). The outlier screen should eliminate implausibly large wages that are likely to reflect typographical errors, but it should also remove extremely high-wage individuals (e.g., professional athletes and some entertainers are covered by workers' compensation) whose wages are recorded accurately. Exclusion of such high-wage individuals is motivated purely by statistical considerations, since extreme outliers can be so influential on the average that information about the majority of workers is not discernible. If such outliers appear only occasionally, they can make estimation of trends in lost earnings much more difficult.

That said, the choice of an outlier threshold is inherently subjective, and our choice of $1 million annual earnings arguably leaves scope for high-wage workers to drive the trends. We therefore conducted sensitivity analyses by estimating trends in wage loss that use a lower threshold ($100,000 quarterly earnings) and a higher threshold ($1 million quarterly earnings). Relative to our main estimation sample, raising the outlier threshold to $1 million per quarter adds 171 injured workers to our sample, while lowering the outlier threshold to $100,000 per quarter removes 1,735 injured workers from the sample.

Relative earnings by period (pre-recession, recession, post-recession) under these alternative outlier criteria are presented in Table B.10 alongside our main estimates. We find that trends in quarterly earnings losses are practically identical under these alternative outlier screens. While $400,000 annualized earnings is still a high wage (particularly relative to the population of workers' compensation claimants), the stability of our estimates makes us confident that our

Table B.10
Sensitivity of WCIS Earnings Loss Estimates to Threshold for Earnings Outliers

	Injury Year 2005–2007	Injury Year 2008–2009	Injury Year 2010–2012
Main sample (< $250,000 quarterly earnings)			
Relative earnings, second post-injury year (%)	74.48	67.12	65.99
Injured worker earnings, second post-injury year	$21,521	$17,940	$18,128
Control worker earnings, second post-injury year	$29,161	$26,986	$27,717
Loose outlier threshold (< $1 million quarterly earnings)			
Relative earnings, second post-injury year (%)	74.44	67.24	66.08
Injured worker earnings, second post-injury year	$21,572	$18,045	$18,190
Control worker earnings, second post-injury year	$29,241	$27,101	$27,779
Strict outlier threshold (< $100,000 quarterly earnings)			
Relative earnings, second post-injury year (%)	74.14	66.88	65.64
Injured worker earnings, second post-injury year	$21,237	$17,644	$17,830
Control worker earnings, second post-injury year	$28,896	$26,628	$27,394

NOTE: Injured workers are excluded as outliers if they have total quarterly earnings in any quarter of their wage history above the outlier threshold.

choice of outlier screens did not drive our main results. A nontrivial number of workers (just over 0.5 percent of the otherwise eligible sample) are removed by our stricter outlier screen, and we are concerned that lower thresholds would begin to undermine the representativeness of our data.

Earnings Loss Estimates Stratified by Firm Size and Industry

In light of concerns about the representativeness of our data sources for workers' compensation claims, we conducted two exercises to assess the robustness of our estimated wage loss trends to differential non-reporting of claims to the WCIS by industry and firm size.

There are two reasons to be concerned about the ability of our data to capture earnings losses at small employers. First, some analysts suspect that reporting of workers' compensation administrative data to claims databases tends to overrepresent large employers. Second, our control-worker methodology depends on the availability of coworkers who match the injured worker's pre-injury wage and job tenure, and so the probability of match failure is mechanically higher at small firms. At the limit, it is impossible to find an uninjured control worker for an injured worker at a one-person firm (many of which are covered under both UI and workers' compensation in California).

In our main analysis, we corrected for match failure using an inverse propensity score method applied in previous RAND studies.[9] Under the assumption that, among workers injured at the same-size firm with similar wages in the same quarter, match failure is uncorrelated with earnings loss, this method delivers estimates that are representative of the popula-

---

[9]   See Bhattacharya et al. (2010) for a discussion of our previous use of this method, and see Little and Rubin (1987) for further technical details. We used the quartile of the weekly wage interacted with firm size and quarter of injury fixed effects as the covariates in the model used to predict match failure.

Methods and Supplemental Results for Chapter Five

Estimation of Statutory Benefits for WCIS

Due to several limitations of the information on PPD ratings and benefits available in the WCIS, our analysis of trends in statutory benefits combines data from the DEU and the WCIS to predict the average final rating and benefits for WCIS cases as a function of data observable in the WCIS. Although it would be ideal to use individual-level data on actual disability ratings and benefits to analyze replacement rates, it is not possible to observe these outcomes for recent injury cohorts in either the DEU or the WCIS. The key limitation of the DEU for analyzing trends in benefits is that the population of DEU cases becomes less representative for recent injury years. As discussed in Chapter Six, this is because severe and complex cases can take five or more years to reach the DEU. Furthermore, as noted above, the population of workers captured in the DEU differs systematically from the population observed in the WCIS, and so wage loss estimates from the DEU may not represent the experience of the average PPD claimant in the state.

Meanwhile, the WCIS also has limitations that make it difficult to analyze trends in ratings and benefits using WCIS data alone. As noted in Chapters Three and Five, the WCIS does not have sufficiently detailed or reliable information on PD ratings to calculate statutory PPD benefits. The WCIS does have the advantage of reporting amounts of PPD benefits paid to date, and it is believed that paid-to-date amounts in WCIS are accurate. Without more detailed or reliable data on ratings, however, it is not generally possible to know whether PPD payments on a case have been completed. Because PPD benefits may be paid over many years or, for severe cases eligible for life pensions, until the worker's death, paid-to-date amounts reported in the WCIS are likely to understate the total value of benefit payments that will eventually be made to the average worker. In principle, paid-to-date amounts on closed cases should capture the total amount of benefits. However, slightly less than half (48 percent) of WCIS cases with PPD payments are reported as being closed at the time of data extraction, and this percentage also declines sharply in recent years. Table C.1 presents estimates of relative earnings, wage loss, paid amounts, and estimated statutory benefits for closed versus open cases in the WCIS. The table stratifies cases on date of injury to account for the portion of cases that are closed, which also highlights the difficulty of using closed cases to measure recent trends. As measured by earnings losses, closed cases are dramatically less severe, and the differences between closed and open cases grows as we examine more recent injuries and the right-truncation problem becomes more severe. The choice between using paid amounts on all claims or restricting attention to closed claims thus represents a dilemma in which either approach may lead to biased estimates of trends in benefit levels due to right-censoring.

Table C.1
Wage Losses and Statutory Benefits for Closed Versus Open Cases, by Date of Injury

	Injury Year 2005–2007		Injury Year 2008–2009		Injury Year 2010–2012	
	Closed	Not Closed	Closed	Not Closed	Closed	Not Closed
Relative Earnings, Second Post-Injury Year (%)	73.3	74.5	68.1	65.1	71.6	61.5
Projected Five-Year Earnings Loss	$33,412	$38,728	$38,161	$47,630	$34,825	$52,932
S.B. 899 Statutory Benefits	$16,993	$28,545	$18,009	$29,694	$16,478	$28,278
PPD Paid to Date	$11,892	$11,174	$12,273	$12,265	$9,109	$8,459

NOTES: Table contains 2005–2012 injuries reported in WCIS. Claim status and paid-to-date amounts measured as of September 2014. Statutory benefits estimated using matched WCIS-DEU sample as described below, with predicted benefits reweighted under the assumption that 74 percent of cases are represented as per WCIRB (2015). All dollar amounts reported in constant 2014 dollars.

In order to estimate trends in ratings, benefit levels, and replacement rates in a way that is consistent over time, we use a subset of claimants appearing in both the WCIS and DEU to model final ratings and statutory benefits as a function of data elements appearing in the WCIS. We then use this model to predict statutory benefits for all cases appearing in the WCIS, allowing us to analyze replacement rate trends for all workers in the WCIS. The critical assumption underlying this approach is that, after controlling for the observable characteristics of a case, the unobservable determinants of a WCIS case's final rating do not vary systematically with whether or not a case is evaluated at the DEU (i.e., there is no selection on unobservables).

This assumption is not directly testable, but its content depends on the set of variables from WCIS that are included in our model. Since the goal of the model is to predict final ratings and benefits on the basis of incomplete information from the WCIS, we include variables intended to capture the nature and severity of the worker's injury, as well as other factors (including residence in Southern California, where claimants are differentially likely to be represented by an applicant's attorney, and whether a case is closed).[1] We also include flexible gender-specific age profiles to capture age adjustments in the rating process and potential gender-specific differences in the distribution of detailed impairments within body parts of injury. Our preferred specification uses the following case characteristics to predict the final rating at the DEU, all entered as sets of dummy variables:

• receipt of TTD benefits and deciles of estimated TTD duration
• body part of injury codes reported on the FROI
• pre-injury annual earnings
• age in years interacted with gender
• claim status (closed versus open) interacted with residence in Southern California.

---

[1] We used three-digit zip codes of residence as reported in the DEU data (with missing values assigned from linked WCIS data where possible) to rank the counties of California by the fraction of DEU ratings with representation. After examining the fraction represented for all three-digit zip codes in California, we defined "Southern California" to include all three-digit zip codes in California between 900 and 935, excluding zip codes 919, 920, 921, and 934. Roughly speaking, this area comprises the greater Los Angeles region and inland areas in Fresno or further south, and excludes coastal areas outside of Ventura, Los Angeles, and Orange Counties. This definition is similar to the "L.A. Basin" region defined by WCIRB but includes a larger portion of inland California where representation was more common among DEU cases.

Formally, this regression model can be expressed as follows

$$B_{isc} = \alpha_{sc} + X_i \beta^X + \varepsilon_{isc}$$

where B_{isc} is the real discounted present value of statutory benefits after apportionment for individual i in region s with WCIS claim status c injured in year t, X_i contains data on demographics and injury characteristics observed in the WCIS, and α_{sc} represents an intercept that varies flexibly depending on whether the claimant lives in Southern California (s = 1) or elsewhere (s = 0) and whether the case was closed (c = 1) or open (c = 0) at the time that data was extracted from the WCIS.[2] This model captures variation in the level of statutory benefits that is systematically related to features of a case observable in the WCIS.

TTD receipt and duration are strongly associated with statutory benefits, with statutory benefits increasing steadily with TTD duration. Benefits also vary widely (up to $45,000) with the body part of injury after controlling for other worker and case characteristics. The body parts of injury associated with the highest statutory benefits are multiple body systems (which includes polytrauma), the heart, the internal organs, and the spinal cord, while the body parts of injury associated with the lowest statutory benefits are the toes, nose, thumb, fingers, and knee. Benefits also increase with age for both male and female workers.[3] Finally, there were sizable differences in statutory benefits associated with geography and WCIS claim status, even after controlling for the other factors mentioned here. Open cases in Southern California had statutory benefits that were $4,300 higher than similar open cases elsewhere in California, while closed cases were associated with statutory benefits that were approximately $2,500 (in Southern California) to $3,600 (elsewhere in California) higher than open cases in the same region, reflecting the fact that more severe cases remain open longer. While this regression model explains only 14 percent of the variation in statutory benefits, we do not need to have high explanatory power for the model to accomplish its goal of yielding unbiased predictions of statutory benefits based on characteristics observed in the WCIS.

We use the estimated coefficients from the above regression model to predict statutory benefits for all cases in the WCIS as a function of case characteristics, defining $\hat{B}^X(X_{isc})$ as follows

---

[2] We model benefits directly rather than modeling ratings and then computing benefits on the basis of predicted ratings because, holding wages constant, benefits are a convex function of ratings. Modeling benefits based on predicted ratings would lead to an underestimate of benefits due to Jensen's inequality, which holds that a convex function of the expectation of a random variable is necessarily less than the expectation of a convex function of a random variable. Similarly, we explored models that used the natural log of statutory benefits as the dependent variable, but while these models fit the data slightly better than our preferred model, predicted benefit levels from these models were biased substantially downward due to Jensen's inequality.

[3] We explored models that also incorporated permanent impairment and PD rating information from the WCIS. Even though these variables are often placeholders estimated for insurance reserving purposes early in the life of a claim, they were strongly predictive of statutory benefits. However, we found that these models were not appropriate for modeling time trends, as PD rating information in the WCIS also appeared to be subject to right-censoring problems that tend to bias trends downward in recent years. Body part of injury, in contrast, is available shortly following the date of injury on the FROI. As discussed in Appendix B, right-censoring is more of a concern with TTD duration, but we think this is unlikely to affect our estimates substantially because we use deciles of TTD duration, and the 80th percentile of implied TTD duration (approximately 72.5 weeks) is somewhat below the duration between the last injury dates in our sample and the time of data collection (approximately 89 weeks). Furthermore, as discussed in Appendix B, downward trends in TTD duration for PPD cases following the recession are apparent across the severity distribution, and not just in the right tail of cases that would be affected by right-censoring.

$$\hat{B}^X(X_{isc}) = \hat{\alpha}_{sc} + X_i \hat{\beta}^X$$

$\hat{B}^X(X_{isc})$ captures the average relationship between injury characteristics and final ratings over all available cases from the 2005–2012 injury years, but it does not capture two of the most important influences on ratings: injury date and time between the injury and the DEU rating. Besides the strong relationship between time to rating and case severity that led to the right-censoring problems discussed in Chapters Five and Six, injury date has an independent effect on ratings that must be accounted for to provide an accurate description of trends in ratings and benefits. As described in Chapter Five, this "ratings creep" may reflect the gradual accumulation of expertise about the rating system on the part of doctors and applicants' attorneys. While we do not need to understand its origins, we do need to factor time effects into our predicted ratings. In particular, we need to estimate time effects in a way that captures trends among high-maturity cases as well as low-maturity cases.

We accomplish this by estimating a separate regression model that adds dummy variables for year of injury (i.e., time effects) to the main specification described just above. This model includes cases at all available maturities and deals with right-censoring by controlling flexibly for case maturity at rating (in 100-day bins of time between the injury and DEU rating). This specification assumes that time effects on benefits are additively separable from the effect of time to rating on ratings (denoted here M_i) and benefits. Put differently, we assume that time effects shift the entire maturity curve in parallel. This model can be expressed as follows:

$$X_{isct} = \alpha^T_{sc} + X_i \beta^{TX} + M_i \gamma^T + \varphi^T_{sct} + \eta_{isct}$$

The objective of this model is to isolate the profile of time effects φ^T_{sct}, which are allowed to vary freely with WCIS case status (c) and residence in Southern California (s). The time effects capture trends in benefits holding constant case characteristics and the time between injury and rating. Because $\hat{B}^X(X_{isc})$ already contains an intercept term capturing the long-run average level of benefits for the years 2005–2012, we de-mean the estimated time effects by subtracting off the in-sample average $\bar{\hat{\varphi}}^T_{sct}$ and then add the de-meaned time profile to the predicted value $\hat{B}^X(X_{isc})$ based on injury characteristics so that the predicted statutory benefits also capture the time trend in benefits caused by ratings creep.

$$\hat{B}(X_{isct}) = \hat{B}^X(X_{isc}) + (\hat{\varphi}^T_{sct} - \bar{\hat{\varphi}}^T_{sct})$$

We estimate $\hat{B}(X_{isct})$ stratified on type of DEU rating to capture the distinct trends in ratings for represented and unrepresented cases separately. The resulting predicted values have a reasonably good in-sample fit among the sample of matched DEU-WCIS cases used to estimate the model, as shown in Table C.2.

Under an assumption about the fraction of cases that are represented, we can calculate a prediction for the average WCIS case. As elsewhere in this report, we assume that 74 percent of cases are represented in each injury year for 2005–2012 as per estimates from WCIRB (2015). To produce the estimates presented in Chapter Five, we use a weighted average of $\hat{B}(X_{isct})$ for represented and unrepresented cases where the weight assigned to represented cases is fixed at 74 percent in all quarters of injury.

Table C.5
Worker Characteristics of DEU Versus WCIS Wage Loss Samples

Demographics	WCIS	DEU
Average age	44.4	46.1
Percent female	42	40
Pre-injury annual earnings (2014$)	$46,083	$50,086
Industry		
Accommodations/food service (%)	5	4
Administrative/support (%)	6	5
Agriculture (%)	3	3
Construction (%)	7	7
Education (%)	5	10
Health care (%)	8	9
Manufacturing (%)	13	11
Other (%)	16	16
Public administration (%)	13	19
Retail (%)	13	9
Transport/warehousing (%)	5	5
Wholesale (%)	6	5
Unweighted number of cases with matched controls	345,282	88,668

NOTES: WCIS wage loss sample consists of WCIS claims with matched wage histories and matched controls. DEU wage loss sample consists of constant-maturity claims rated within 899 days of injury (thus comparable through 2011) and with matched wage histories and matched controls.

pre-injury annual earnings are about $4,000 higher for DEU workers in constant 2014 dollars ($50,086 for DEU cases versus $46,083 for WCIS cases).

Differences in the industrial composition of the DEU population versus the WCIS population are also apparent. The most striking differences are driven by different coverage of public employers in the two databases. The fraction of cases with an industry code in the Public Administration sector is 19 percent in the DEU, versus 13 percent in the WCIS. Education, another sector with substantial public employment, accounts for 10 percent of the DEU caseload versus 5 percent of the WCIS caseload.[7] To the extent that employment in Public Administration and Education is correlated with public-sector employment, these workers may enjoy greater job security and experience better return to work. These differences are offset by higher shares of workers in Retail and Manufacturing in the WCIS.

We cannot know with certainty whether the WCIS or the DEU is more representative of the industrial mix for the overall population of PPD cases in California. The WCIS is known to suffer from a nontrivial amount of underreporting on subsequent reports of injury, which

---

[7] The industry data from EDD that we use consist only of NAICS codes, which do not distinguish between public- and private-sector establishments. In 2012, the public administration industry (NAICS code 92) encompassed only about 36 percent of government employment in California: a larger share of public employees worked in education (44 percent). Health care, another industry with substantial public-sector employment, accounts for 9.5 percent of DEU cases versus 8.4 percent for WCIS.

contain the information on benefit receipt that we use to define the PPD population. Some analysts familiar with the WCIS have suggested that there is differentially greater underreporting of public-sector injuries, in which case the DEU could be more representative of the true PPD population than the WCIS. We addressed this concern by estimating wage loss trends that stratify the WCIS on industry and reweight according to statewide employment changes. The results of this calculation, presented in Appendix Figure B.3, strongly resemble the main estimates presented in Chapter Four.

Table D.1
Proportional Earnings, Injured Earnings, and Control Earnings by Final Rating, 2005–2008 DEU Cases

Final Rating Before Apportionment	Year 1 (Loss) (%)	Year 2 (Loss) (%)	Year 3 (Loss) (%)	Year 4 (Loss) (%)	Year 5 (Loss) (%)	Ratio of Five-Year Losses to Second-Year Losses (%)
0–4	14.6	7.3	6.4	6.7	7.2	5.76
5–9	19.9	12.7	10.9	10.4	11.1	5.12
10–14	27.8	21.1	18.9	18.7	18.9	4.99
15–19	33.3	27.9	25.5	24.7	25.3	4.90
20–29	39.8	37.0	34.8	33.0	33.8	4.82
30–100	50.6	54.8	54.5	54.3	53.6	4.88
All Ratings	30.4	26.3	24.8	24.3	24.6	4.95

Injured Worker Annual Earnings

Final Rating Before Apportionment	Year 1 (Injured)	Year 2 (Injured)	Year 3 (Injured)	Year 4 (Injured)	Year 5 (Injured)	Number of Cases
0–4	$37,930	$39,433	$38,329	$36,651	$35,362	12899
5–9	$34,308	$35,432	$34,567	$33,273	$32,054	17282
10–14	$29,886	$30,480	$29,675	$28,209	$27,040	13449
15–19	$27,239	$27,152	$26,413	$25,069	$23,868	10187
20–29	$24,344	$23,220	$22,506	$21,507	$20,229	11335
30–100	$21,402	$17,552	$15,922	$14,561	$13,747	15936
All Ratings	$29,334	$28,986	$27,980	$26,618	$25,469	81088

Control Worker Annual Earnings

Final Rating Before Apportionment	Year 1 (Controls)	Year 2 (Controls)	Year 3 (Controls)	Year 4 (Controls)	Year 5 (Controls)	Number of Cases
0–4	$44,132	$42,544	$41,032	$39,501	$38,412	12899
5–9	$42,372	$40,582	$38,999	$37,478	$36,561	17282
10–14	$40,615	$38,625	$36,975	$35,418	$34,333	13449
15–19	$39,792	$37,665	$35,999	$34,368	$33,396	10187
20–29	$39,018	$36,872	$35,338	$33,687	$32,691	11335
30–100	$41,082	$38,874	$37,095	$35,652	$34,577	15936
All Ratings	$41,314	$39,349	$37,724	$36,179	$35,157	81088

ship and then test for the equality of coefficients across models. Ordinary least squares (OLS) regression of the relationship between earnings loss and benefits using microdata on earnings losses is inconsistent, however. As discussed in Chapter Three, individual earnings losses are subject to severe measurement error induced by sampling error in control worker earnings. The problem is not that control earnings are measured with error: the EDD earnings data are likely the most accurate possible measure of covered wages in existence. The problem, rather, is that the average outcome for a finite number of control workers is a very noisy measure of any individual worker's true earnings potential. This sampling error is not problematic when earn-

Table D.2
Proportional Earnings, Injured Earnings, and Control Earnings by Selected Impairment, 2005–2008 Single-Impairment DEU Cases

Hand or finger impairment (16.05.xx.xx or 16.06.xx.xx)

Final Rating Before Apportionment	Year 1 (Loss) (%)	Year 2 (Loss) (%)	Year 3 (Loss) (%)	Year 4 (Loss) (%)	Year 5 (Loss) (%)	Ratio of Five-Year Losses to Second-Year Losses
0–4	5.7	1.4	2.6	1.7	1.1	9.03
5–9	11.4	2.3	3.1	3.7	5.5	11.16
10–14	18.8	8.7	5.3	5.2	7.5	5.23
15–19	24.1	13.6	7.0	5.1	9.5	4.34
20–29	34.3	30.3	32.8	31.9	38.7	5.55
30–100	41.2	38.3	18.5	11.1	18.2	3.32
All Ratings	10.3	3.9	4.0	3.5	4.2	6.70

Injured Worker Annual Earnings

Final Rating Before Apportionment	Year 1 (Injured)	Year 2 (Injured)	Year 3 (Injured)	Year 4 (Injured)	Year 5 (Injured)	Number of Cases
0–4	$36,871	$36,949	$34,979	$33,810	$33,103	2247
5–9	$33,692	$34,245	$32,130	$30,203	$28,756	1068
10–14	$29,264	$29,484	$28,410	$26,770	$25,142	495
15–19	$29,466	$29,226	$29,146	$27,138	$25,126	196
20–29	$24,445	$24,128	$24,713	$22,605	$21,209	100
30–100	$23,347	$22,716	$28,690	$28,582	$24,064	25
All Ratings	$34,403	$34,593	$32,892	$31,414	$30,304	4131

Control Worker Annual Earnings

Final Rating Before Apportionment	Year 1 (Controls)	Year 2 (Controls)	Year 3 (Controls)	Year 4 (Controls)	Year 5 (Controls)	Number of Cases
0–4	$39,019	$37,464	$35,941	$34,428	$33,505	2247
5–9	$37,695	$35,066	$33,229	$31,506	$30,693	1068
10–14	$35,347	$32,300	$30,135	$28,442	$27,576	495
15–19	$37,615	$33,845	$31,512	$28,856	$28,327	196
20–29	$36,301	$34,598	$36,054	$33,649	$34,582	100
30–100	$38,502	$36,808	$35,492	$32,660	$30,754	25
All Ratings	$38,101	$35,980	$34,334	$32,662	$31,831	4131

Knee impairment (17.05.xx.xx)

Final Rating Before Apportionment	Year 1 (Loss) (%)	Year 2 (Loss) (%)	Year 3 (Loss) (%)	Year 4 (Loss) (%)	Year 5 (Loss) (%)	Ratio of Five-Year Losses to Second-Year Losses (%)
0–4	14.9	4.7	3.5	4.5	4.9	6.94
5–9	18.7	6.8	3.9	3.3	3.9	5.37
10–14	23.4	14.3	15.5	18.1	17.7	6.22
15–19	29.2	21.9	23.9	24.9	25.4	5.72
20–29	29.9	26.0	26.4	27.5	31.5	5.43
30–100	37.0	39.7	45.0	52.2	56.3	5.80
All Ratings	19.7	10.0	9.2	10.1	10.8	5.95

Table D.2—Continued

Injured Worker Annual Earnings

Final Rating Before Apportionment	Year 1 (Injured)	Year 2 (Injured)	Year 3 (Injured)	Year 4 (Injured)	Year 5 (Injured)	Number of Cases
0–4	$42,676	$46,158	$45,002	$42,744	$41,183	3721
5–9	$38,873	$42,455	$41,800	$40,285	$38,896	2908
10–14	$37,750	$40,180	$37,469	$34,603	$33,651	1341
15–19	$33,770	$34,546	$31,730	$29,093	$27,393	694
20–29	$32,686	$32,147	$30,254	$27,714	$24,175	577
30–100	$30,146	$27,498	$22,820	$18,175	$15,818	272
All Ratings	$39,205	$41,953	$40,464	$38,235	$36,659	9513

Control Worker Annual Earnings

Final Rating Before Apportionment	Year 1 (Controls)	Year 2 (Controls)	Year 3 (Controls)	Year 4 (Controls)	Year 5 (Controls)	Number of Cases
0–4	$49,890	$48,416	$46,677	$44,907	$43,550	3721
5–9	$47,373	$45,553	$43,569	$41,811	$40,653	2908
10–14	$48,738	$46,896	$44,756	$43,079	$41,974	1341
15–19	$46,701	$44,236	$42,293	$40,118	$38,617	694
20–29	$45,688	$43,451	$41,743	$39,678	$37,846	577
30–100	$47,005	$45,578	$43,331	$41,955	$41,487	272
All Ratings	$48,388	$46,639	$44,741	$42,952	$41,677	9513

Carpal tunnel syndrome impairment (16.01.02.02)

Final Rating Before Apportionment	Year 1 (Loss) (%)	Year 2 (Loss) (%)	Year 3 (Loss) (%)	Year 4 (Loss) (%)	Year 5 (Loss) (%)	Ratio of Five-Year Losses to Second-Year Losses (%)
0–4	16.0	9.9	7.7	8.7	6.5	4.94
5–9	18.1	13.6	12.6	13.3	15.7	5.38
10–14	21.3	13.3	20.3	18.8	14.8	6.67
15–19	19.6	19.2	22.1	25.2	18.0	5.41
20–29	30.1	29.3	36.5	45.8	35.5	6.05
30–100	Insufficient Data					
All Ratings	18.2	13.1	13.1	14.1	13.2	5.48

Injured Worker Annual Earnings

Final Rating Before Apportionment	Year 1 (Injured)	Year 2 (Injured)	Year 3 (Injured)	Year 4 (Injured)	Year 5 (Injured)	Number of Cases
0–4	$35,639	$36,525	$36,317	$34,959	$35,131	404
5–9	$34,329	$34,685	$33,909	$32,678	$30,952	538
10–14	$33,493	$34,870	$31,800	$30,622	$30,466	149
15–19	$32,454	$30,712	$27,866	$24,207	$25,762	70
20–29	$24,252	$22,546	$20,715	$18,475	$19,734	46
30–100	Insufficient Data					
All Ratings	$33,919	$34,374	$33,353	$31,917	$31,329	1216

Table D.2—Continued

Final Rating Before Apportionment	Year 1 (Controls)	Year 2 (Controls)	Year 3 (Controls)	Year 4 (Controls)	Year 5 (Controls)	Number of Cases
Control Worker Annual Earnings						
0–4	$42,141	$40,534	$39,458	$38,503	$37,747	404
5–9	$41,589	$40,145	$38,950	$38,008	$37,256	538
10–14	$42,059	$40,202	$39,963	$38,198	$36,408	149
15–19	$39,905	$38,030	$36,278	$33,782	$32,612	70
20–29	$33,861	$31,881	$32,344	$33,079	$31,037	46
30–100	Insufficient Data					
All Ratings	$41,133	$39,550	$38,551	$37,485	$36,537	1216

Low back pain impairment (15.03.01.00 or 15.03.02.02)

Final Rating Before Apportionment	Year 1 (Loss) (%)	Year 2 (Loss) (%)	Year 3 (Loss) (%)	Year 4 (Loss) (%)	Year 5 (Loss) (%)	Ratio of Five-Year Losses to Second-Year Losses (%)
0–4	24.2	15.9	12.3	13.8	16.8	5.22
5–9	20.0	13.6	10.4	7.5	7.9	4.37
10–14	27.7	22.3	18.3	17.5	17.5	4.63
15–19	34.5	28.8	25.2	22.9	23.9	4.70
20–29	38.2	35.2	33.6	32.5	33.0	4.90
30–100	55.2	56.9	55.6	50.3	50.0	4.71
All Ratings	30.8	25.9	22.9	20.8	21.2	4.69

Injured Worker Annual Earnings

Final Rating Before Apportionment	Year 1 (Injured)	Year 2 (Injured)	Year 3 (Injured)	Year 4 (Injured)	Year 5 (Injured)	Number of Cases
0–4	$35,433	$34,448	$34,772	$34,795	$31,999	155
5–9	$29,913	$30,506	$30,333	$29,960	$29,095	3486
10–14	$27,963	$27,957	$27,732	$26,630	$25,511	3373
15–19	$26,748	$26,896	$26,584	$25,869	$24,893	2540
20–29	$26,539	$25,918	$24,819	$23,643	$22,610	1978
30–100	$19,789	$16,538	$15,771	$15,698	$15,167	862
All Ratings	$27,560	$27,418	$27,020	$26,276	$25,291	12394

Control Worker Annual Earnings

Final Rating Before Apportionment	Year 1 (Controls)	Year 2 (Controls)	Year 3 (Controls)	Year 4 (Controls)	Year 5 (Controls)	Number of Cases
0–4	$45,362	$40,965	$39,820	$40,450	$38,895	155
5–9	$36,962	$35,301	$34,011	$32,625	$31,867	3486
10–14	$37,915	$35,973	$34,331	$32,919	$31,803	3373
15–19	$39,767	$37,760	$36,098	$34,508	$33,904	2540
20–29	$41,799	$39,987	$38,250	$36,626	$35,794	1978
30–100	$40,998	$38,407	$37,141	$35,009	$34,387	862
All Ratings	$38,954	$37,022	$35,493	$33,993	$33,157	12394

Table D.2—Continued

Final Rating Before Apportionment	Year 1 (Loss) (%)	Year 2 (Loss) (%)	Year 3 (Loss) (%)	Year 4 (Loss) (%)	Year 5 (Loss) (%)	Ratio of Five-Year Losses to Second-Year Losses (%)
Digestive system impairment (06.xx.00.xx)						
0–4	12.9	15.0	18.7	13.2	10.2	4.67
5–9	31.4	30.8	30.6	31.6	30.2	5.02
10–14	33.8	30.6	37.9	29.8	40.9	5.65
15–19	35.9	38.8	38.0	46.4	48.5	5.35
20–29	41.7	43.1	48.8	53.7	57.2	5.67
30–100	49.0	54.8	35.2	34.7	24.3	3.61
All Ratings	35.5	36.5	35.9	36.8	37.6	4.99

Injured Worker Annual Earnings

Final Rating Before Apportionment	Year 1 (Injured)	Year 2 (Injured)	Year 3 (Injured)	Year 4 (Injured)	Year 5 (Injured)	Number of Cases
0–4	$33,391	$31,314	$28,618	$29,013	$31,126	23
5–9	$34,623	$32,285	$30,677	$29,104	$28,271	70
10–14	$27,895	$26,086	$22,749	$23,471	$18,402	56
15–19	$31,745	$26,151	$25,709	$20,750	$19,437	59
20–29	$20,351	$17,683	$15,451	$12,930	$11,528	59
30–100	$20,755	$19,985	$23,855	$21,830	$24,691	39
All Ratings	$28,225	$25,512	$24,308	$22,410	$21,292	306

Control Worker Annual Earnings

Final Rating Before Apportionment	Year 1 (Controls)	Year 2 (Controls)	Year 3 (Controls)	Year 4 (Controls)	Year 5 (Controls)	Number of Cases
0–4	$38,132	$36,831	$35,507	$33,887	$34,890	23
5–9	$49,272	$46,667	$44,970	$43,848	$42,354	70
10–14	$40,606	$37,610	$37,020	$34,662	$33,780	56
15–19	$47,104	$42,757	$41,974	$40,608	$40,185	59
20–29	$33,298	$31,076	$30,614	$29,630	$29,299	59
30–100	$42,398	$44,201	$39,413	$37,184	$35,439	39
All Ratings	$42,475	$40,196	$38,750	$37,203	$36,407	306

Shoulder impairment 16.02.01.xx or 16.02.02.xx

Final Rating Before Apportionment	Year 1 (Loss) (%)	Year 2 (Loss) (%)	Year 3 (Loss) (%)	Year 4 (Loss) (%)	Year 5 (Loss) (%)	Ratio of Five-Year Losses to Second-Year Losses (%)
0–4	18.5	8.9	5.8	7.3	8.8	5.52
5–9	21.8	13.0	11.8	12.2	14.0	5.61
10–14	26.9	16.7	13.8	14.3	15.2	5.20
15–19	32.0	26.5	25.8	26.2	27.5	5.21
20–29	36.5	34.0	33.0	34.0	36.5	5.11
30–100	47.6	47.2	48.2	48.1	49.4	5.09
All Ratings	25.6	17.5	15.7	16.4	17.9	5.31

Table D.2—Continued

Final Rating Before Apportionment	Year 1 (Injured)	Year 2 (Injured)	Year 3 (Injured)	Year 4 (Injured)	Year 5 (Injured)	Number of Cases
Injured Worker Annual Earnings						
0–4	$35,704	$38,361	$38,142	$36,228	$34,676	2079
5–9	$35,778	$37,944	$36,722	$35,124	$33,317	2450
10–14	$32,266	$34,979	$34,477	$32,731	$31,142	1866
15–19	$30,100	$30,968	$29,756	$27,474	$25,805	1404
20–29	$27,775	$26,293	$25,291	$23,370	$21,115	767
30–100	$25,658	$21,918	$19,788	$17,180	$15,712	221
All Ratings	$33,154	$34,878	$34,045	$32,177	$30,468	8787

Control Worker Annual Earnings

Final Rating Before Apportionment	Year 1 (Controls)	Year 2 (Controls)	Year 3 (Controls)	Year 4 (Controls)	Year 5 (Controls)	Number of Cases
0–4	$43,488	$42,120	$40,596	$39,288	$38,369	2079
5–9	$45,273	$43,593	$41,860	$40,426	$39,414	2450
10–14	$43,578	$42,002	$40,277	$38,725	$37,540	1866
15–19	$43,572	$42,128	$40,608	$38,499	$37,395	1404
20–29	$42,317	$39,866	$38,435	$36,938	$35,686	767
30–100	$45,440	$41,546	$39,807	$37,147	$36,225	221
All Ratings	$43,965	$42,296	$40,674	$39,101	$38,041	8787

Psychiatric impairment (14.01.00.00)

Final Rating Before Apportionment	Year 1 (Loss) (%)	Year 2 (Loss) (%)	Year 3 (Loss) (%)	Year 4 (Loss) (%)	Year 5 (Loss) (%)	Ratio of Five-Year Losses to Second-Year Losses (%)
0–4	37.6	35.2	43.0	42.3	36.4	5.53
5–9	45.4	33.5	36.5	25.3	22.8	4.88
10–14	51.1	45.3	37.4	37.1	34.7	4.54
15–19	49.1	47.6	40.3	39.0	37.7	4.49
20–29	58.2	58.8	53.6	50.5	47.6	4.57
30–100	62.5	67.6	66.1	65.9	63.7	4.82
All Ratings	56.1	56.2	52.6	50.6	48.3	4.70

Injured Worker Annual Earnings

Final Rating Before Apportionment	Year 1 (Injured)	Year 2 (Injured)	Year 3 (Injured)	Year 4 (Injured)	Year 5 (Injured)	Number of Cases
0–4	$21,640	$20,787	$18,340	$15,778	$15,760	34
5–9	$20,776	$23,214	$20,547	$21,143	$21,138	186
10–14	$19,848	$19,400	$20,086	$19,382	$20,039	287
15–19	$20,306	$18,326	$18,611	$17,497	$16,705	321
20–29	$17,140	$14,553	$15,422	$15,296	$15,215	484
30–100	$16,169	$12,465	$10,863	$10,069	$9,848	758
All Ratings	$18,052	$15,926	$15,402	$14,823	$14,690	2070

Table D.2—Continued

Final Rating Before Apportionment	Year 1 (Controls)	Year 2 (Controls)	Year 3 (Controls)	Year 4 (Controls)	Year 5 (Controls)	Number of Cases
Control Worker Annual Earnings						
0–4	$33,701	$32,069	$32,135	$29,337	$27,423	34
5–9	$36,625	$34,920	$33,291	$29,986	$29,108	186
10–14	$37,969	$35,487	$33,350	$32,549	$32,364	287
15–19	$37,504	$34,995	$32,715	$31,140	$29,914	321
20–29	$37,683	$35,306	$34,334	$33,111	$32,026	484
30–100	$40,182	$38,433	$36,253	$35,384	$34,332	758
All Ratings	$38,449	$36,340	$34,519	$33,217	$32,252	2070
Final Ratings Before Apportionment Used						

ings are an outcome variable, but it leads to very severe classical measurement error if earnings are used as an explanatory variable. OLS estimation of this relationship yields a coefficient of 0.062 [95% confidence interval 0.0552–0.0687], which might seem to suggest that an additional dollar of earnings loss leads to only an additional 6 cents of compensation.

Instead, we use the impairment rating as an instrumental variable for earnings loss in a regression of statutory benefits on earnings loss. Instrumental variables regression is a statistical method that, in our application, isolates the variation in earnings losses that is predicted by an impairment rating system and asks whether this variation translates into benefits. The instrumental variables regression coefficient therefore summarizes in a single number the overall relationship between losses and benefits under a policy regime and can be interpreted as a quantitative measure of vertical equity. This approach is analogous to estimating a line of best fit through the grouped data points in Figures 6.4 and 6.5, but it allows us to avoid arbitrary choices about the level of aggregation and perform valid statistical inference on the resulting estimates. Estimates are sensitive to the level of aggregation because the relationship between earnings losses and benefits is nonlinear.

Instrumental variables (IV) methods allow consistent estimation in the presence of measurement error as long as noise in the instrument is uncorrelated with noise in the explanatory variable of interest (Hausman, 2001). Impairment ratings satisfy this condition unless idiosyncratic variation in an injured worker's impairment rating is correlated with the labor market outcomes of his controls.

To be clear, these IV estimates do not have a causal interpretation. Benefits are mechanically linked to the impairment rating, so it clearly does not meet the exclusion restriction necessary for a valid instrumental variable. The model used here can, nonetheless, serve as a test of vertical equity under the following argument: if the rating system did not, on average, assign higher benefits to workers with greater earnings losses, the instrumental variables estimate would be zero. If we estimate a non-zero coefficient, then the system must assign higher benefits to cases with higher earnings losses.

Estimation of Horizontal Equity Measures

To measure the degree of horizontal equity, we estimate a linear regression model where the explanatory variables are the final rating and interactions between the final rating and the impairment category. We use the F-statistic on the interaction terms to measure the magnitude of differences across body parts of injury in the level of earnings loss and in the relationship between ratings and earnings loss. Importantly for our purposes (because the dependent variable differs under S.B. 899 and S.B. 863 due to different cases being grouped together), the F-statistic is normalized by the amount of variation in the dependent variable. The F-statistic under S.B. 863 (F = 94.1) was slightly higher than the F-statistic under S.B. 899 (F = 91.8).

We are not aware of statistical theory regarding the difference between two F-statistics, so we used a permutation method to derive p-values for our test statistic treating the rating system in effect (S.B. 899 or S.B. 863) as the binary treatment to be permuted (Good, 2006). For the seven impairment categories presented in Figures 6.6–6.7, we constructed permutation datasets in which we exchanged ratings (and cell-average earnings losses) calculated under S.B. 899 with ratings and earnings losses calculated under S.B. 863. For the analysis of selected impairments, there was a small number of permutations (128) so we enumerated all permutations to obtain critical values for our test statistic. The difference between the two F-statistics was near the center of the permutation distribution (two-sided p-value = 0.9375), leading us to conclude that, among the conditions examined in Chapter Six, the implementation of S.B. 863 did not lead to a change in horizontal equity that was distinguishable from chance. Sensitivity analyses that excluded psychiatric impairments and cases with ratings of 30 or higher also yielded no evidence that S.B. 863 led to a statistically significant change in horizontal equity.

Abbreviations

AMA	American Medical Association
AME	agreed medical evaluator
BLS	Bureau of Labor Statistics
CHSWC	California Commission on Health and Safety and Workers' Compensation
DEU	California Disability Evaluation Unit
DIR	Department of Industrial Relations
DWC	Division of Workers' Compensation
EDD	California Employment Development Department
EDI	Electronic Data Interchange
FEC	future earnings capacity
FROI	First Report of Injury
GAF	Global Assessment of Functioning
MMI	maximum medical improvement
NAICS	North American Industry Classification System
P&S	permanent and stationary
PD	permanent disability
PDRS	Permanent Disability Rating Schedule
PPD	permanent partial disability
QCEW	Quarterly Census of Earnings and Wages
QME	qualified medical evaluator
S.B.	Senate Bill
SJDB	Supplemental Job Displacement Benefit
SROI	Subsequent Report of Injury
SAWW	Statewide Average Weekly Wage
SSN	Social Security number
TTD	total temporary disability

UI	unemployment insurance
WCAB	Workers' Compensation Appeals Board
WCIRB	Workers' Compensation Insurance Rating Bureau
WCIS	Workers' Compensation Information System

References

Altman, B., "Disability Definitions, Models, Classification Schemes, and Applications," in G. L. Albrecht, K. D. Seelman, and M. Bury, eds., *Handbook of Disability Studies*, Thousand Oaks, Calif.: Sage Publications, 2001.

Anderson, Patricia M., Bruce D. Meyer, John Pencavel, and Mark J. Roberts, "The Extent and Consequences of Job Turnover," *Brookings Papers on Economic Activity. Microeconomics*, 1994, pp. 177–248. doi:10.2307.2534731.

Asfaw, A., R. Pana-Cryan, and R. Rosa, "The Business Cycle and the Incidence of Workplace Injuries: Evidence from the U.S.A.," *Journal of Safety Research*, Vol. 42, No. 1, 2011, pp. 1–8.

Azaroff, Lenore S., Charles Levenstein, and David H. Wegman, "Occupational Injury and Illness Surveillance: Conceptual Filters Explain Underreporting," *American Journal of Public Health*, Vol. 92, No. 9, 2002, pp. 1421–1429. doi:10.2105/AJPH.92.9.1421.

Berkowitz, M., and J. F. Burton, Jr., *Permanent Disability Benefits in Workers' Compensation*, Kalamazoo, Mich: W. E. Upjohn Institute for Employment Research, 1987.

Bhattacharya, J., F. Neuhauser, R. T. Reville, and S. A. Seabury, "Evaluating Permanent Disability Ratings Using Empirical Data on Earnings Losses," *Journal of Risk and Insurance*, Vol. 77, No. 1, 2010, pp. 231–260.

BLS BDM. BLS Business Employment Dynamics. As of January 9, 2016: http://www.bls.gov/bdm/sizeclassqanda.htm

Boden, L. I., and M. Galizzi, "Economic Consequences of Workplace Injuries and Illnesses: Lost Earnings and Benefit Adequacy," *American Journal of Industrial Medicine*, Vol. 36, No. 5, 1999, pp. 487–503.

———, "Income Losses of Women and Men Injured at Work," *Journal of Human Resources*, Vol. 38, No. 3, 2003, pp. 722–757.

Boone, J., and J. C. van Ours, "Are Recessions Good for Workplace Safety?" *Journal of Health Economics*, Vol. 25, No. 6, 2006, pp. 1069–1093.

Boone, J., J. C. van Ours, J.-P. Wuellrich, and J. Zweimüller, "Recessions Are Bad for Workplace Safety," *Journal of Health Economics*, Vol. 30, No. 4, 2011, pp. 764–773.

Bureau of Labor Statistics, "Labor Force Statistics from the Current Population Survey (Seas) Employment Level—Part-Time for Economic Reasons, All Industries," 2015. As of September 13, 2015: http://data.bls.gov/timeseries/LNS12032194

Butler, R. J., W. G. Johnson, and M. L. Baldwin, "Managing Work Disability: Why First Return to Work Is Not a Measure of Success," *Industrial & Labor Relations Review*, Vol. 48, No. 3, 1995, pp. 452–469.

Cheadle, A., G. Franklin, C. Wolfhagen, J. Savarino, P. Liu, C. Salley, and M. Weaver, "Factors Influencing the Duration of Work-Related Disability: A Population-Based Study of Washington State Workers' Compensation," *American Journal of Public Health*, Vol. 84, No. 2, 1994, pp. 190–196.

Cocchiarella, L., and G. B. J. Andersson, eds., *Guides to the Evaluation of Permanent Impairment*, 5th ed., Chicago: American Medical Association, 2001.

Currie, J., and B. C. Madrian, "Health, Health Insurance and the Labor Market," *Handbook of Labor Economics*, Vol. 3, 1999, pp. 3309–3416.

Davidson, Russell, and James G. MacKinnon, *Estimation and Inference in Econometrics*, Oxford: Oxford University Press, 1993.

Division of Workers' Compensation, *Schedule for Rating Permanent Disabilities*, California, Labor and Workforce Development Agency, Department of Industrial Relations, 2005.

Elsby, M. W., B. Hobijn, and A. Şahin, *The Labor Market in the Great Recession*, Washington, D.C.: National Bureau of Economic Research, 2010.

Fishback, P. V., and S. E. Kantor, *The Adoption of Workers' Compensation in the United States 1900–1930*, Washington, D.C.: National Bureau of Economic Research, 1996.

Galizzi, M., and L. I. Boden, *What Are the Most Important Factors Shaping Return to Work?: Evidence from Wisconsin*, Cambridge, Mass.: Workers Compensation Research Institute, 1996.

Good, P. I., *Permutation, Parametric, and Bootstrap Tests of Hypotheses*, New York: Springer Science & Business Media, 2006.

Gunderson, M., and Hyatt, D., *Some Benefit Considerations in Workers' Compensation*, Toronto: Royal Commission on Workers' Compensation in British Columbia, 1998.

Hausman, J., "Mismeasured Variables in Econometric Analysis: Problems from the Right and Problems from the Left," *Journal of Economic Perspectives*, Vol. 15, No. 4, 2001, pp. 57–67.

Ho, D. E., K. Imai, G. King, and E. A. Stuart, "Matching as Nonparametric Preprocessing for Reducing Model Dependence in Parametric Causal Inference," *Political Analysis*, Vol. 15, No. 3, 2007, pp. 199–236.

Hoynes, Hilary, Douglas L. Miller, and Jessamyn Schaller, "American Economic Association Who Suffers During Recessions?" *The Journal of Economic Perspectives*, Vol. 26, No. 3, 2012, pp. 27–47.

Hunt, H. A., "Benefit Adequacy in State Workers' Compensation Programs," *Social Security Bulletin-Washington*, Vol. 65, No. 4, 2004, p. 24.

Hunt, H. A., and R. V. Habeck, *The Michigan Disability Prevention Study: Research Highlights*, Kalamazoo, Mich: W. E. Upjohn Institute for Employment Research, 1993.

Lee, Myoung-jae, *Micro-Econometrics for Policy, Program, and Treatment Effects*, Oxford: Oxford University Press, 2005.

Little, R. J. A., and D. B. Rubin, *Statistical Analysis with Missing Data*, New York: John Wiley, 1987.

Livermore, G. A., and T. C. Honeycutt, "Employment and Economic Well-Being of People with and Without Disabilities Before and after the Great Recession," *Journal of Disability Policy Studies*, Vol. 26, No. 2, September 2015, pp. 70–79.

McLaren, Christopher F., Robert T. Reville, and Seth A. Seabury, *How Effective are Employer Return to Work Programs?* Santa Monica, Calif.: RAND Corporation, WR-745-CHSWC, 2010. As of May 3, 2016: http://www.rand.org/pubs/working_papers/WR745.html

Mendeloff, John, Christopher Nelson, Kilkon Ko, and Amelia M. Haviland, *Small Businesses and Workplace Fatality Risk: An Exploratory Analysis*, Santa Monica, Calif.: RAND Corporation, TR-371-ICJ, 2006. As of May 3, 2016: http://www.rand.org/pubs/technical_reports/TR371.html

National Academy of Social Insurance (NASI), *Adequacy of Earnings Replacement in Workers' Compensation Programs*, Kalamazoo, Mich.: W. E. Upjohn Institute for Employment Research, 2004.

National Commission, *The Report of the National Commission on State Workmen's Compensation Laws*, Washington, D.C.: The National Commission on State Workmen's Compensation Laws, 1972.

Neuhauser, F. W., "Analysis of Ratings Under the New PD Schedule, through June 30, 2007," a memorandum to Christine Baker at CHSWC and Dave Bellusci at WCIRB, August 8, 2007.

Peterson, Mark A., Robert T. Reville, Rachel Kaganoff Stern, and Peter S. Barth, *Compensating Permanent Workplace Injuries: A Study of the California System*, Santa Monica, Calif.: RAND Corporation, 1998. As of May 3, 2016: http://www.rand.org/pubs/monograph_reports/MR920.html

Reinhart, Carmen M., and Kenneth S. Rogoff, "Recovery from Financial Crises: Evidence from 100 Episodes," *American Economic Review: Papers & Proceedings*, Vol. 104, No. 5, 2014, pp. 50–55.

Reville, Robert T., Leslie I. Boden, Jeff E. Biddle, and Christopher Mardesich, *An Evaluation of New Mexico Workers' Compensation Permanent Partial Disability and Return to Work*, Santa Monica, Calif.: RAND Corporation, 2001. As of May 3, 2016:
http://www.rand.org/pubs/monograph_reports/MR1414.html

Reville, Robert T., and Robert F. Schoeni, *Disability from Injuries at Work: The Effects on Earnings and Employment*, Santa Monica, Calif.: RAND Corporation, 2001. As of May 3, 2016:
http://www.rand.org/pubs/drafts/DRU2554.html

Reville, Robert, Robert Schoeni, and Craig W. Martin, *Trends in Earnings Loss from Disabling Workplace Injuries in California: The Role of Economic Conditions*, Santa Monica, Calif., RAND Corporation, 2002. As of May 3, 2016:
http://www.rand.org/pubs/monograph_reports/MR1457.html

Reville, Robert T., Seth A. Seabury, Frank W. Neuhauser, John F. Burton, Jr., and Michael D. Greenberg, *An Evaluation of California's Permanent Disability Rating System*, Santa Monica, Calif.: RAND Corporation, 2005. As of May 3, 2016:
http://www.rand.org/pubs/monographs/MG258.html

Seabury, Seth A., Robert T. Reville, and Frank W. Neuhauser, *Data for Adjusting Disability Ratings to Reflect Diminished Future Earnings and Capacity in Compliance with S.B. 899*, Santa Monica, Calif.: RAND Corporation, 2004. As of May 3, 2016:
http://www.rand.org/pubs/working_papers/WR214.html

Seabury, Seth A., Robert T. Reville, Stephanie Williamson, Christopher F. McLaren, Adam Gailey, Elizabeth Wilke, and Frank W. Neuhauser, *Workers' Compensation Reform and Return to Work*, Santa Monica, Calif.: RAND Corporation, 2011. As of May 3, 2016:
http://www.rand.org/pubs/monographs/MG1035.html

Seabury, Seth A., and Ethan Scherer, *Identifying Permanently Disabled Workers with Disproportionate Earnings Losses for Supplemental Payments*, Santa Monica, Calif.: RAND Corporation, 2013. As of May 3, 2016:
http://www.rand.org/pubs/research_reports/RR425.html

Sengupta, I., M. L. Baldwin, and V. P. Reno, *Workers' Compensation: Benefits, Coverage, and Costs, 2012*, Washington, D.C.: National Academy of Social Insurance, 2014.

Silverstein, M., "Meeting the Challenges of an Aging Workforce," *American Journal of Industrial Medicine*, Vol. 51, 2008, pp. 269–280.

Studdert, David M., Michelle M. Mello, Atul A. Gawande, Tejal K. Gandhi, Allen Kachalia, Catherine Yoon, Ann Louise Puopolo, and Troyen A. Brennan, "Claims, Errors, and Compensation Payments in Medical Malpractice Litigation," *The New England Journal of Medicine*, Vol. 354, 2006, 2024–2033, doi:10.1056/NEJMsa054479.

Summers, L. H., "US Economic Prospects: Secular Stagnation, Hysteresis, and the Zero Lower Bound," *Business Economics*, Vol. 49, No. 2, 2014, pp. 65–73.

U.S. Chamber of Commerce, *2012 Analysis of Workers' Compensation Laws*, Washington, D.C., 2012.

WCIRB, *Analysis of Changes in Indemnity Claim Frequency—2013 Report*, Oakland, Calif.: Workers' Compensation Insurance Rating Bureau of California, 2013.

———, *Actuarial Committee Meeting, Review of Diagnostics, Exhibit E7, August 6*, Oakland, Calif.: Workers' Compensation Insurance Rating Bureau of California, 2015.